CASH FLOW AND CORPORATE FINANCE IN VICTORIAN BRITAIN

CASES FROM THE BRITISH COAL INDUSTRY
1860–1914

CASH FLOW AND CORPORATE FINANCE IN VICTORIAN BRITAIN

CASES FROM THE BRITISH COAL INDUSTRY
1860–1914

by

T.J. Baldwin, R.H. Berry, R.A. Church
and M.V. Pitts

UNIVERSITY
of
EXETER
PRESS

First published in 2000 by
University of Exeter Press
Reed Hall, Streatham Drive
Exeter EX4 4QR
UK
www.ex.ac.uk/uep/

The authors gratefully acknowledge financial support
from the ESRC (Grant 234513) in collecting
the financial data for this book.

British Library Cataloguing in Publication Data
A catalogue record for this book is available
from the British Library.

ISBN 0 85989 651 X

Printed in Great Britain by
Short Run Press Ltd, Exeter

CONTENTS

PART 1

1 INTRODUCTION

This study focuses on joint stock limited liability companies in the coal, iron and steel industries, which comprised a major and rapidly expanding sector of the economy during the mid and late Victorian period and one in which company formation was a relatively early development following the mid century legislation. Generalizations concerning finance and performance in this sector have not been tested by any systematic analysis of corporate accounts, except at the level of an individual enterprise. Yet Cottrell's assertion that 'The joint stock companies that were established in both the coal and iron industries were generally unsuccessful' (Cottrell 1980: 34) remains unchallenged. It also begs the question as to the criteria to be used in reaching such a judgment. Elsewhere the authors have analysed the profitability of a single firm employing various criteria, though paying particular attention to a contemporary measure of what informed commentators regarded as a satisfactory expected rate of return in these industries (Church, Baldwin and Berry 1994: 703–724).

Using a sample population of between twenty and thirty companies, depending on the specific questions posed and the availability of adequate archival material, our ultimate aim is to generalize, with greater quantitative precision than has been attempted hitherto, on levels of profitability, but also on other aspects of the history of business finance in the British coal, iron and steel industries between 1860 and 1914. What were the sources of business finance and their relative size? What dividend policies were adopted? What were the trends, changes and differences, in these respects, not only over time but between companies, and is it possible to identify structural as well as cyclical factors which might account for such differences? None of these questions is novel, though historians' investigations so far have tended to focus on individual companies, or on the history of a few over short periods, and have asked only one or two of those questions. The novelty of our approach is to examine the records of a comparatively large number of companies whose history extended over several decades, and to try to answer a wide range of questions based on annual data over a long period. Before it is feasible to attempt this, however, it is necessary to assemble data in accordance with the requirements of a methodology which will answer these questions.

The purpose of this monograph, therefore, is to present an

examination of the feasibility of developing and applying a methodology which is based on the concept of *cash flow* rather than *flow of funds*, the approach which has characterized the research of some previous investigators, for example, T.A. Lee (1978) and Edwards and Webb (1982). The results of this application which are presented in tabular form below are, therefore, an intermediate outcome of a larger project. By emphasizing cash flow it is intended to complement contemporary balance sheets to produce financial statements which are both more consistent and more in tune with modern accounting practice. The presentation of these statements is a necessary precondition to enable us to tackle the substantive historical questions referred to above. The data set contained in the second part of this monograph is the basis on which subsequent analysis of the kind outlined above may take place, not only by the authors but by other scholars. Those interested in the history of the coal, iron and steel industries may find the data and the commentary which precedes it of most value. However, the methodology we have used is equally applicable to other companies and to other industries. To that extent, the methodology explained with reference to the transformation of the accounts of a single firm only, Consett (see Baldwin, Berry and Church 1992), provides a key to the systematic historical analysis of firms and industries on a common comparative basis such as that which we present below.

The justification for adopting this highly labour-intensive approach in analysing company accounts must be a conviction that the figures presented provide sufficient detail to sustain confident interpretation and generalization, and that they are credible. These are considerations which must be examined before proceeding to a substantive explanation of our methodology in section 4 and the data sets which follow.

Many writers have contributed to a well-established body of criticism of nineteenth-century company accounts including: Brief (1965), G.A. Lee (1975), T.A. Lee (1978), Marriner (1980) and Wale (1990). In general, the nature of such criticism is twofold. Firstly, that no compulsory standard existed in law, at the time of their publication, as to the form and content of such accounts and, secondly, that no general agreement existed as to the accounting principles and practices to be adopted in their preparation. Of late, however, this criticism has been tempered by the views of authors such as Parker (1991) and Arnold (1995), the former, in particular, urging business historians, 'not to discard accounts but to learn more about them'.

In order to place this debate in context, sections 2 and 3 of this monograph examine, in turn, the corporate and accounting environments in which the financial reports forming the basis of this study were originally prepared and presented. Section 4 outlines the methodology adopted in the formulation of the cash flow statements presented in Part 2, while section 5 seeks to emphasize and explain the differing nature of profit and cash for the benefit of economic historians who may not be entirely familiar with these concepts as applied in an accounting context.

2 THE CORPORATE ENVIRONMENT

Yamey (1960) contended that many of the conventions upon which modern financial reporting was based have their origins in the Victorian era. The timing of this development is not surprising. Following the industrial revolution a cheap and easy means of access to capital markets was essential to success in business. In manufacturing and mining this was initially provided through partnerships, the survival of which depended heavily upon trust. The gradual transition from business conducted through partnership and trust to corporate enterprise based on contract began with the Joint Stock Companies Act of 1844 which for the first time in Britain allowed incorporation by the relatively simple means of 'registration' (although not, at that stage, with the added benefit of limited liability). Prior to this, the only means of company formation was via the very cumbersome route of either Royal Charter (chartered companies) or Act of Parliament (statutory companies). The genesis of financial reporting convention through the second half of the nineteenth century is inextricably linked with the development of the legislation relating to the joint stock company.

The Joint Stock Companies Act 1844
In 1841 a Select Committee on Joint Stock Companies was established, in response to a growing concern over fraud, which was seen as one result of the state of the law relating to business ownership and finance. Fraud among large unregistered and unregulated joint stock partnerships abounded, and included, 'the making up of fraudulent accounts . . . facilitated sometimes by the accounts not being audited' (British Parliamentary Papers 1844: VII, p. ix). One of the Committee's conclusions was that 'periodical accounts, if honestly made and fairly audited, cannot fail to excite attention to the real state of a concern; and by means of improved remedies, parties to mismanagement may be made more amenable for acts of fraud and illegality' (*ibid*: VII, p. v).

This conclusion was to shape the accounting clauses to be included in the Joint Stock Companies Act 1844, clauses which, in the view of Edey and Panitpakdi (1956: 356), were 'surprisingly modern in outlook'. The major accounting and associated provisions of the Act were as follows:

1. Books of account were to be kept, and periodically balanced.

2.   A 'full and fair' balance sheet was to be presented at each ordinary meeting; a copy having previously been sent to every shareholder.

3.   Auditors were to be appointed to report on each balance sheet; such report to be read at the relevant meeting.

4.   The audited balance sheet was to be filed with the Registrar of Joint Stock Companies.

Notably absent from the Act, however, was either a prescription as to the form and content of the proposed balance sheet, or a requirement for the provision of a profit and loss account.

The Limited Liability Act 1855 and Joint Stock Companies Act 1856
The right to register a joint stock company with the benefit of limited liability was first introduced by the Limited Liability Act 1855. This privilege, however, was not extended to banks until 1858, nor to insurance companies until 1870. Even then, a special duty was imposed on such companies to publish half-yearly statements of assets and liabilities, together with details of authorized, issued, and called-up share capital. From this stage the accounting and auditing requirements of such concerns were effectively decoupled from those of ordinary commercial companies which, until the turn of the century, were to become the subject of a far less stringent financial reporting regime. As Parker (1990: 69) pointed out, however, for the greater part of the nineteenth century regulated[1] companies rather than joint stock companies 'constituted in value terms the major part of the corporate private sector'. Furthermore, he concluded that Edey's view that prior to 1900 there was a 'complete absence of statutory regulation in matters relating to accounting and audit' (1956: 223), while true for commercial and industrial companies, did not apply to the economy as a whole.

In 1856 a new Joint Stock Companies Act came on to the statute book, replacing both the 1844 and 1855 Acts. The concept of limited liability was reaffirmed within the new Act, but surprisingly the compulsory accounting and auditing requirements of the 1844 Act were abandoned. Instead, a set of model 'articles of association' were included within Table B of the 1856 Act (later to become Table A of the Companies Act 1862) which were to be adopted where a company did not register its own alternative clauses.

Under the terms of the 1856 Act, therefore, the adoption of the model articles of association was entirely optional; a company was able to pick and choose which, if any, of the provisions contained within Table B it might wish to incorporate into its own articles of association. In practice, however, even for commercial and industrial companies, the regulatory situation after 1856 may not have been as bleak in all cases as

---

1. 'Regulated companies' in this context include 'railways, the public utilities (gas, electricity, water) the banks, the insurance companies and other financial institutions' (Parker 1990: 52).

might at first appear. In their study of the Wigan Coal and Iron Company Limited (WCI), for example, Edwards and Webb (1982: 271) noted that, 'The directors drew heavily on the provisions of Table A of the Companies Act 1862 when designing WCI's articles of association.' Thus, while in Britain in the latter half of the nineteenth century there may not have been a global framework of financial regulation in place, it would be untrue to say that *no* regulatory framework existed. For this reason it is necessary, particularly in the case of 'non-regulated companies', to consider the constitution (contained in the articles of association) of each individual company in turn to establish how far accounting and auditing rules extended and drew upon the model clauses contained in Table B.

Table B of the Joint Stock Companies Act 1856

Clauses 69 to 84 of Table B of the Joint Stock Companies Act 1856, those relating to accounting and auditing matters, are reproduced in full in Annex 2.1 at the end of this section. Clause 69 set down a framework for the keeping of accounting records and in particular recommended, explicitly for the first time within corporate legislation, that such records be kept 'upon the Principle of Double Entry'.[2] This is particularly interesting in view of the fact that the first item of which the clause suggests 'true' account should be kept is that 'Of the Stock in Trade of the Company', which is of course a notoriously difficult matter under the double entry system. In general the clause seems to give pride of place to the capture and recording of trading type transactions (stock, receipts, expenditures) and less emphasis on the record of the working capital of an enterprise.

Clauses 70 and 71 recommend the publication of an annual 'Statement of Income and Expenditure' and in general terms the items which should be included therein. Particularly interesting in this context is the suggestion that on the income side 'gross Income' should distinguish 'the Several Sources from which it has been derived'. With regard to 'gross Expenditure' the clause is no less forward-thinking, for the sentiment that where expenditure 'may in Fairness be distributed over several Years ... the whole Amount of such Item shall be stated, with the addition of the Reasons why only a Proportion of the Expenditure is charged against the Income of the Year' would be quite acceptable in a modern accounting standard.

In the event, neither the secondary literature nor our own archival research has produced evidence suggesting that clauses 70 and 71 found great favour among early company sponsors. As Jones and Aiken (1994: 227) observed, 'The intimate trading and operating details contained in the profit and loss account were considered too commercially sensitive for public disclosure'. The clauses do, however, show the existence in certain quarters of a fairly sophisticated approach to financial reporting at this time. Furthermore, as Edey and Panitpakdi conjecture, 'the precedent

---

2. A short exposition outlining the main characteristics of the 'double-entry' process is provided in section 3 on page 12.

set by these Tables may have influenced the form of companies' particular articles' (1956: 362).

Clause 72 recommended the publication of an annual balance sheet by the company, while clause 73 suggested that a printed copy of such should be forwarded to each shareholder seven days prior to the meeting. As some indication of the feeling of the times, however, it may be noted that even this seemingly quite innocuous proposal was not without its detractors. For example, in 1869 Charles Markham, the Managing Director of the Staveley Coal and Iron Company, was moved to propose to shareholders attending the AGM that the annual balance sheet should not be distributed to shareholders at all, but simply 'laid upon the table each year' (Staveley Archive: 39/80/12, Minutes of General Meetings No. 1, p. 71). Without doubt the most significant aspect of these clauses, however, is the reference contained in clause 72 to a balance sheet 'in the Form annexed to this Table'. As an indication of the state of the art in financial reporting at that time, the pro-forma balance sheet in question is reproduced in Annex 2.2 at the end of this section.

The balance sheet was presented in the traditional 'English' form with 'PROPERTY AND ASSETS' on the right and 'CAPITAL AND LIABILITIES' on the left. While appearing to conform to the conventional 'reverse order to liquidity', the 'property and assets' side does not distinguish between fixed and current assets, as would be the form in modern accounts, but rather between 'PROPERTY', 'DEBTS' and 'CASH AND INVESTMENTS'. 'Property' was subdivided into immovable and movable property, the former grouping consisting of freehold and leasehold land and buildings while the latter heading brought together, unusually by today's standards, stock in trade and plant. Particularly notable in this section of the balance sheet is the caveat 'The Cost to be stated with Deductions for Deterioration in Value as charged to the Reserve Fund or Profit and Loss'.

In the case of 'Debts owing to the company' another informative sequence is suggested, distinguishing between good debts, secured and unsecured, and debts considered doubtful and bad. Once more, an added caveat 'Any Debt due from a Director or other Officer of the Company to be separately stated' is modern in tone.

Finally, on the assets side of the balance sheet the item 'Cash and Investments' presents information as to the nature of investments and rate of interest thereon. No information as to current market value, either by way of note or otherwise, appears to be required. In the case of cash, however, as well as the need to report whether or not it is interest bearing, there is also a requirement to note where cash is lodged. This item may well reflect a less than complete confidence in the early Victorian banking system.

The ordering of items on the 'capital and liabilities' side of the pro-forma balance sheet is rather less conventional to the modern eye compared with that of the assets side. After an initial section, which showed capital contributed by shareholders in some detail, the amounts of any reserve fund and unappropriated profit and loss account balance were relegated to a position below 'debts and liabilities' to third parties. This formulation is, however, in line with Yamey's (1962b) view that prior to 1889 the nominal paid-up share capital of a company was an important bench-mark: an irreducible minimum below which the value of the company's assets should not, under normal circumstances, be allowed to fall.

The heading 'debts and liabilities' was fully broken down in terms of loans secured by mortgage or debenture and other 'debts' owing by the company. The 'debts' themselves were then further subdivided into no fewer than six separate categories; these included trade creditors, outstanding interest on debentures and loans, and acceptances on bills of exchange. A final caveat which required details to be given of any contingent liabilities against the company completed the 'capital and liabilities' side of the balance sheet.

With regard to the clauses relating to 'audit' (clauses 74–84), Edey and Panitpakdi's (1956: 366) observation is relevant: 'Any student of company accounting law will be struck by [their] remarkably modern ring.' Apart from the references in clause 84 to a 'full and fair' balance sheet exhibiting a 'true and correct' state of affairs, perhaps the most notable departure from present practice is the empowerment of the auditor to employ, at the company's expense through clause 83, 'Accountants or other Persons to assist him'. It should be remembered that at this time there was no specific requirement that an auditor be other than a lay person, so long as he was not a 'Director or other Officer of the Company' (clause 76). Thus, in appraising the 'regulatory framework' relevant to a particular company at this time the quality and professional status of its auditor may prove to be a matter of some relevance.

The Companies Acts 1862 and 1900

The Companies Act 1862 was mainly consolidatory, bringing together company legislation previously enacted into one statute. No material change was made to the voluntary accounting and auditing provisions contained in Table B of the 1856 Act, which now became Table A of the Companies Act 1862. Interestingly, one minor but significant omission from the new Act was the requirement, originally contained in clause 69 of Table B, that accounts be kept, 'upon the Principle of Double Entry'.

During the second half of the nineteenth century a dramatic increase in the number of registered companies occurred, rising from 2,000 in 1864 to nearly 9,000 companies in 1884 and over 60,000 by 1914 (Edwards 1989: 105). Yet no further significant changes in accounting and auditing requirements for ordinary commercial and industrial companies occurred until the Companies Act 1900. Surprisingly, this Act made no change to the *voluntary* nature of the accounting reporting provisions contained in the 1862 Act, though for the first time since 1856 the Act introduced the requirement for an annual audit of all registered companies to be carried out, 'and thereby imposed, by inference, an obligation to prepare an annual balance sheet' (Edey and Panitpakdi 1956: 372).

Review

At first glance, Edey's view of nineteenth-century corporate financial reporting following the the Joint Stock Companies Act 1856 as being typified by a 'complete absence of statutory regulation in matters relating to accounting and audit' (1956: 223) appears to be a plausible assessment. It would be a mistake, however, to assume that, simply because no *mandatory* accounting regulation existed at that time, *no* process of financial reporting was taking place. Section 4 will show that, while few companies took up the voluntary accounting and auditing clauses set out in Table B of the 1856 Act, at an operational level most appear to have adopted their own form of regulations (Edwards and Webb 1985). Perhaps surprisingly, therefore, in the light of the statutory environment described in this section the major problem in the analysis of nineteenth-century corporate financial statements is not the lack of financial reporting data available, but rather the possibility of a total lack of any consistency or comparability in such data, either between companies, or within the same company over time.

With a view to examining the extent of this problem, the next section outlines the development of the financial reporting process throughout the second half of the nineteenth century in response to growing demands from the users of financial information. In particular, the section focuses on the problems of accounting for fixed assets giving rise to the creation of so-called nineteenth-century 'accounting error' (Brief 1965), a source of much recent criticism.

Annex 2.1.
Joint Stock Companies Act 1856 Table B (Sections 69–84)

69. The Directors shall cause true Accounts to be kept,—

Of the Stock in Trade of the Company;

Of the Sums of Money received and expended by the Company, and the Matter in respect of which such Receipt and Expenditure takes place; and,

Of the Credits and Liabilities of the Company:

Such Accounts shall be kept, upon the Principle of Double Entry, in a Cash Book, Journal, and Ledger: The Books of Account shall be kept at the principal Office of the Company, and subject to any reasonable Restrictions as to the Time and Manner of inspecting the same that may be imposed by the Company in General Meeting, shall be open to the Inspection of the Shareholders during the Hours of Business.

70. Once at the least in every Year the Directors shall lay before the Company in General Meeting a Statement of the Income and Expenditure for the past Year, made up to a Date not more than Three Months before such Meeting.

71. The Statement so made shall show, arranged under the most convenient Heads, the Amount of gross Income, distinguishing the Several Sources from which it has been derived, and the Amount of gross Expenditure, distinguishing the Expense of the Establishment, Salaries, and other like Matters: Every Item of Expenditure fairly chargeable against the Year's Income shall be brought into Account, so that a just Balance of Profit and Loss may be laid before the Meeting; and in Cases where any Item of Expenditure which may be distributed over several Years has been incurred in any One Year the whole Amount of such Item shall be stated, with the addition of the Reasons why only a Portion of such Expenditure is charged against the Income of the Year.

72. A Balance Sheet shall be made out in every Year, and laid before the General Meeting of the Company, and such Balance Sheet shall contain a Summary of the Property and Liabilities of the Company arranged under the Heads appearing in the Form annexed to this Table, or as near thereto as Circumstances admit.

73. A printed Copy of such Balance Sheet shall, Seven Days previously to such Meeting, be delivered at or sent by Post to the registered Address of every Shareholder.

74. The Accounts of the Company shall be examined and the Correctness of the Balance Sheet ascertained by One or more Auditor or Auditors to be elected by the Company in General Meeting.

75. If not more than One Auditor is appointed, all the Provisions herein contained relating to Auditors shall apply to him.

76. The Auditors need not be Shareholders in the Company: No Person is eligible as an Auditor who is interested otherwise than as a Shareholder in any Transaction of the Company; and no Director or other Officer of the Company is eligible during his Continuance in Office.

77. The Election of Auditors shall be made by the Company at their Ordinary Meeting, or, if there are more than One, at their First Ordinary Meeting in each Year.

78. The Remuneration of the Auditors shall be fixed by the Company at the Time of their Election.

79. Any Auditor shall be re-eligible on his quitting Office.

80. If any casual Vacancy occurs in the Office of Auditor, the Directors shall forthwith call an Extraordinary General Meeting for the Purpose of supplying the same.

81. If no Election of Auditors is made in manner aforesaid, the Board of Trade may, on the Application of One Fifth in Number of the Shareholders of the Company, appoint an Auditor for the current Year, and fix the Remuneration to be paid to him by the Company for his Services.

82. Every Auditor shall be supplied with a Copy of the Balance Sheet, and it shall be his Duty to examine the same, with the Accounts and Vouchers relating thereto.

83. Every Auditor shall have a List delivered to him of all Books kept by the Company, and he shall at all reasonable Times have Access to the Books and Accounts of the Company: He may, at the Expense of the Company, employ Accountants or other Persons to assist him in investigating such Accounts, and he may in relation to such Accounts examine the Directors or any other Officer of the Company.

84. The Auditors shall make a Report to the Shareholders upon the Balance Sheet and Accounts, and in every such Report they shall state whether, in their Opinion, the Balance Sheet is a full and fair Balance Sheet, containing the Particulars required by these Regulations, and properly drawn up so as to exhibit a true and correct View of the State of the Company's Affairs, and in case they have called for Explanations or Information from the Directors, whether such Explanations or Information have been given by the Directors, and whether they have been satisfactory; and such Report shall be read, together with the Report of the Directors, at the Ordinary Meeting.

Annex 2.2.
Joint Stock Companies Act 1856 Table B (pro-forma balance sheet)

C.47.	19° & 20° VICTORIÆ.	A.D. 1856.

Joint Stock Companies. (Table B.)

FORM of BALANCE SHEET referred to in TABLE B.

Dr. BALANCE SHEET of the _____ Co. made up to _____ 18 **Cr.**

CAPITAL AND LIABILITIES

£ s. d.   £ s. d.

I. CAPITAL

Showing:
1. The total Amount received from the Shareholders; showing also:
   (a) The Number of Shares.
   (b) The Amount paid per Share.
   (c) If any Arrears of Calls, the Nature of the Arrear, and the Names of the Defaulters.
   Any Arrears due from any Director or Officer of the Company to be separately stated.
   (d) The Particulars of any forfeited Shares.

II. DEBTS AND LIABILITIES of the Company

Showing:
2. The Amount of Loans on Mortgage or Debenture Bonds.
3. The Amount of Debts owing by the Company, distinguishing—
   (a) Debts for which Acceptances have been given.
   (b) Debts to Tradesmen for Supplies of Stock in Trade or other Articles.
   (c) Debts for Law Expenses.
   (d) Debts for Interest on Debentures or other Loans.
   (e) Unclaimed Dividends.
   (f) Debts not enumerated above.

VI. RESERVE FUND

Showing:
The Amount set aside from Profits to meet Contingencies.

VII. PROFIT AND LOSS

Showing:
The disposable Balance for Payment of Dividend, &c.

CONTINGENT LIABILITIES

Claims against the Company not acknowledged as Debts.
Monies for which the Company is contingently liable.

PROPERTY AND ASSETS

£ s. d.   £ s. d.

III. PROPERTY held by the Company

Showing:
4. Immoveable Property, distinguishing
   (a) Freehold Land.
   (b)   „   Buildings.
   (c) Leasehold „.
5. Moveable Property, distinguishing
   (d) Stock in Trade.
   (e) Plant.
   The Cost to be stated with Deductions for Deterioration in Value as charged to the Reserve Fund or Profit and Loss.

IV. DEBTS owing to the Company

Showing:
6. Debts considered good for which the Company hold Bills or other Securities.
7. Debts considered good for which the Company hold no Security.
8. Debts considered doubtful and bad.
Any Debt due from a Director or other Officer of the Company to be separately stated.

V. CASH AND INVESTMENTS

Showing:
9. The Nature of Investment and Rate of Interest.
10. The Amount of Cash, where lodged, and if bearing Interest.

3 THE DEVELOPMENT OF FINANCIAL REPORTING

Financial accounting before 1844

Although examples of rudimentary double entry bookkeeping procedures in use in Britain prior to 1600 exist, 'relatively few systems were in operation before the late eighteenth century' (Edwards 1989: 57). Prior to widespread adoption of double entry the most commonly used method of accounting was some form of 'charge and discharge' (essentially recording and reporting cash receipts and payments) which had developed out of the English feudal society 'at least as far back as the early thirteenth century' (Yamey 1962a: 15).

Thus, at the time of the industrial revolution (conventionally assigned to the period 1760–1830) a choice of single or double entry accounting systems was available to the industrialist. Not surprisingly, where new industries developed out of the old landed estates, for example mines, iron works and canals, the tendency was to remain loyal to the charge and discharge system employed by the manorial stewards of the past. The difficulties with such a system are, however, well rehearsed. No record of capital invested in the enterprise is readily available and, since no distinction is made between capital and revenue expenditure, no clear indication of 'profit' or 'assets' can easily be deduced. On a more practical level, the recording of credit transactions and the resultant indication of money owed and owing (creditors and debtors) which is provided automatically by the double entry system, is absent in charge and discharge. Over time, therefore, the double entry system came to dominate although, as Edwards (1989: 58) points out, the choice between the two systems was not always clear cut; 'hybrid' systems could be found employing elements of both single and double entry.

The gradual adoption of double entry techniques during the seventeenth and eighteenth centuries however, did not, of itself, necessarily lead to an improvement in standards of record keeping and profit measurement. A study by Yamey (1962a) of surviving ledgers of the period reveals a catalogue of errors and inaccuracies including:

1.   the omission of major assets and liabilities;
2.   the non-closure of some nominal ledger accounts to the profit and loss account;
3.   profit and loss accounts drawn up so as to include items of

11

personal expenditure, capital expenditure and unrealized income;

4.   capital accounts used to dispose of ledger balance which should have been passed through the profit and loss account;

5.   the ignoring, in general terms, of prepayments and accruals;

6.   the use of a so-called 'general account' to dispose of items which should have been accounted for either through the capital account or through the profit and loss account.

These findings led Yamey to conclude that double entry was probably first valued as a *record keeping* device, particularly perhaps for its ability to record and control credit transactions, rather than for its ability to facilitate the measurement of business profit.

Double entry bookkeeping

Before turning to the changes in financial accounting and reporting which took place after 1844 it is important to understand a little of the nature of the double-entry bookkeeping process.

In a single-entry bookkeeping system of charge and discharge, business activity is, in the main, recorded only in so far as it has been translated into receipts and payments of cash. While using such receipts and payments as its 'raw material', the double entry system seeks then to *reclassify* these figures in the form of 'ledger' entries in the manner illustrated in Figure 3.1 below.

Figure 3.1

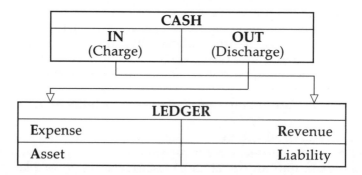

In the ledger, cash receipts are deemed to have been, in the broadest sense, generated either from trading *revenue*: the sale of goods and services, or from borrowing, which will give rise to a *liability* to be repaid at some future time. Rather confusingly, in this somewhat esoteric context, 'borrowing' must include the capital 'borrowed' from the owners of the enterprise (the so-called 'entity concept'). Cash payments, on the other hand, are deemed to relate either to the discharge of *expenses*, resources exhausted in the process of trading, or to the acquisition of *assets*, commodities which are judged to be of some future utility to the enterprise.

From this brief exposition, it is clear that the double entry system allowed management a high degree of discretion particularly, for example, in deciding whether to place a cash payment into a ledger account in quadrant **E** or quadrant **A**. The questionable future utility of expenditure on, say, a new and experimental industrial process, brings this dilemma into sharp relief. The apparent latitude here is, however, combined with a stifling constraint on overall choice which demands that *all* business activity *must* be encapsulated somewhere within what is, in essence, simply a 2 x 2 matrix. This paradox, of highly subjective judgment exercised within a very constrained overall environment, lies at the root of many of the accounting problems which were to manifest themselves in the years after 1844 and which still occur today.

The attractiveness to the early user of the double entry system compared with the charge and discharge model is the considerable utility added even at a record-keeping level. In particular the model is easily extended so as to integrate credit transactions as well as those involving the immediate receipt or payment of cash. In the context of Figure 3.1, for example, a credit sale simply requires an increase in an appropriate ledger account in the **R** quadrant, showing that revenue is *receivable* as a result of that transaction, together with an equal increase in an account in the **A** quadrant to show that an asset, a debtor, now exists. A similar process to record a purchase of goods on credit would require an increase in the **A** quadrant, to show that an asset is now held in the form of stock of one kind or another, together with an equal increase in the **L** quadrant to indicate that a liability, a creditor, is due for payment at some future date.

In due course, a horizontal comparison of ledger accounts classified within the two upper quadrants, **E** and **R**, will form the basis for the preparation of a profit and loss account, while the two lower quadrants, **A** and **L**, will contain the data necessary for the presentation of a balance sheet. Unfortunately, it is in the nature of this process that further accounting adjustments (i.e. reallocation of figures between the four quadrants) are required to deal with such items as closing stock and work in progress, depreciation, accruals, prepayments and bad debts. While not affecting the equilibrium (and thus *apparent* precision) of the double entry model, such accounting allocations add a further element of subjectivity in the accounting process, offering a potential for bias in the resulting financial reports.

The profit and loss account and balance sheet
Throughout the period 1500–1800, according to Chatfield (1977: 69) '[the balance sheet] was by far the most important financial statement'. The reason for this preoccupation with the balance sheet probably stems from

its perceived usefulness as evidence of fulfilment of some 'stewardship function'. For example, a squire and his manorial manager charged with the care and upkeep of the assets entrusted to him would doubtless have found this form of report particularly helpful.

Yamey (1962a: 38) argues forcefully that, prior to 1844, 'calculations of a firm's profits . . . are of little interest to the businessman who is closely and continuously concerned with his own business operations'. Edwards (1989: 77) also takes up this theme making the point that 'the prudent business man [did not] need a formal profit calculation to advise him how much he could afford to spend. He instead based his drawings on the amount of free cash available and adjusted his living standard accordingly'. Finally, Macve (1986) makes the very valid point that in a mediaeval, agricultural economy, with poor communications, alternative investment opportunities would have been severely limited and, in any event, the need for self-sufficiency would, doubtless, outweigh that for profitability. Thus those activities best suited to that end would tend to dominate irrespective of their contribution to profit.

This poses the question concerning the function of the profit and loss account prior to 1844. According to empirical evidence assembled by Yamey (1962a: 23), over the period 1500–1800 the profit and loss account 'served in a weeding-out process, in which detailed and unwanted information in the ledger was removed'. What does Yamey mean by this? The preparation of financial statements using the double entry bookkeeping system involves the need to 'rationalise' the accounts appearing in the ledger from time to time. The function of the profit and loss account in these early times, therefore, probably had far more to do with the closing down of accounts which did not have further financial ramifications, *ex ante*, than with the desire to derive any meaningful measure of profit for the purpose of managerial decision making.

By contrast, in a modern context, this process would generally be carried out by attempting to 'match' past income with the expenditures incurred in generating that income, thereby obtaining a balancing figure purporting to represent some measure of profit or loss on trading activities. The remaining ledger balances not included in this matching process (asset and liability accounts) would be carried down to the ensuing period and subsequently presented in financial reporting terms in the form of a balance sheet. It is generally argued, therefore (Yamey, Edwards), that the modern financial reporting process is 'profit driven', that is to say, the profit and loss account is the report of overriding financial significance, while the balance sheet fulfils a subsidiary role, simply reporting in a systematic manner those balances remaining in the ledger once the profit statement has been compiled.

Financial reporting

The advent of the registered joint stock company in Britain in the mid-nineteenth century, coupled with the introduction of the concept of limited liability, was to cause a sea change in the nature and practice of financial accounting; 'until the coming of general limited liability, it seems that accounting practices were designed to meet the simple requirements of businessmen actively concerned with the management of their own enterprises' (Yamey, 1962a: 38). While hitherto there had been instances of the 'absentee owner', ranging from the 'sleeping partner' in a small firm to a member of one of the giant statutory or chartered companies such as the East India Company, in Yamey's view these arrangements 'had no apparent effect on accounting practice' (*ibid:* 38).

Undoubtedly the most significant factor in financial accounting terms resulting from the emergence of the new limited companies in the latter half of the nineteenth century was the pivotal role assigned to the concept of profit. The reasons for this, in Yamey's view, are twofold. First, particularly in the early years of the joint stock company, the profit figure, however derived, was regarded as setting an upper limit for dividend payments to shareholders, thereby endowing the profit and loss account with a particular financial significance. Second, as absentee owners, shareholders quickly recognized profit as an important indicator of the success and soundness of an enterprise, and of the expertise of its management.[3]

Each of Yamey's explanations deserves further consideration, beginning with the use of profit as an indicator of the amount available for the payment of dividends. It is obvious that, in the final analysis, the payment of dividends was, to a large extent, dependent on the availability of cash (liquid funds) to meet this obligation. For this reason, a prudent company manager in the nineteenth century might have been anxious to try to ensure that reported profits moved, as far as possible, in line with increases in liquidity. For this purpose, therefore, the careful valuation of current assets and liabilities became of paramount importance, whereas increases (or indeed decreases) in the value of fixed assets, in so far as they remained unrealized and did not directly affect liquidity, could be ignored (Pitts: 1998). In these circumstances a rational approach would be to apply as neutral a valuation concept as possible in the appraisal of fixed assets. The 'historic cost' concept (see p. 16 below) widely adopted during the late nineteenth century (Edwards 1989: 111) fits this specification extremely well. In the same way, the general rule that a profit is not recognized until realized in cash or near-cash form probably owes its genesis to a similar approach to business finance which emerged during this period.

When we turn to Yamey's second explanation for the evolution of the concept of profit, the use of profit as an index of management performance, behavioural influences become even more important. The tendency for nineteenth-century joint stock companies to leave profit figures undisturbed by irregular or non-recurring items is, in Yamey's view, perhaps the most tangible indication of managers attempting to

---

3. Recent research by Boyns and Edwards (1977) suggesting a significant increase in the use of financial accounting data for costing purposes during this period may also help to explain the growth in importance of the profit and loss account.

report their performance in the best possible light. Thus, the whole process of 'profit smoothing', whether by the writing-off of certain expenditures over a number of years, depreciation, or by the accumulation of so-called secret reserves (see p. 23 below), may be interpreted as a practical manifestation of company directors' desire for profit stability. The major problem with such policies is that, to a greater or lesser extent, they leave themselves open to a degree of subjective judgment on the part of management which has not always been exercised in the best interests of shareholders or other users of corporate financial reports. For example, the process of creating secret reserves, which is well documented for the late nineteenth and early twentieth centuries, could be masked in respectability by describing it in terms of management's desire to make full and prudent provision for all contingencies. Indeed, it was exactly this course of action upon which the directors of the Staveley Coal and Iron Company, for example, were complimented by the shareholders at the company's 1873 annual general meeting (Staveley Archive: 39/80/12, Minutes of General Meetings No.1, p. 140).

In the case of financial reports a set of rules and conventions, predicated on considerations of self-interest, began to be built up throughout the second half of the nineteenth century.[4] As Yamey points out, these might have been very different had the emerging law relating to corporate affairs (as outlined in the previous section) checked or deflected this development, 'but by and large it had little effect' (Yamey 1962a: 41).

Accounting for fixed assets

We have highlighted the importance of asset valuation in the establishment of a meaningful and workable concept of profit for the newly emerging limited companies during the second half of the nineteenth century. According to Edwards (1989: 82–84), a number of separate and distinctive methods of asset valuation were in operation during the eighteenth and early nineteenth centuries. These included *historic cost*, where fixed assets were retained in the accounting records at their original cost, no charge being made in respect of the contribution of such assets towards current operations. In many instances this method appears to have been used as little more than a simple and objective means of keeping track of an asset's existence. In other cases some attempt was made to provide for depreciation but, according to Edwards, its use 'as a systematic allocation of original cost was slow to appear in business records'.

Apart from this method of fixed asset accounting, which according to Edwards (*ibid:* 83) can be recognized as the forerunner of that used fairly universally by the end of the nineteenth century, other methods fall generally into two categories. In the first, expenditure on fixed assets

---

4. These rules included, incidentally, the four 'fundamental' concepts of accruals, going concern, consistency and prudence, now specified in SSAP 2 (Edwards 1989: 124–5).

would simply have been treated as a current expense and written off against the revenue of the accounting period in which it was incurred. In the main, again according to Edwards, this method tended to be used by small businesses, particularly perhaps those with a history going back to the days of charge and discharge. In their study of the Dowlais Iron Company, however, which they describe as the largest ironworks in the world by 1842 (Edwards and Barber 1979: 139), the authors identify the above treatment of fixed asset expenditure as that which managers referred to then and for another fifty years as 'New Work'.

In the second case, all assets of the business, both fixed and current, were periodically revalued, so that the difference in total net assets at two points in time, duly adjusted for injections and withdrawals of capital, represented some measure of profit for the intervening period. As G.A. Lee (1975: 8) pointed out, 'a modern accountant deals with [the preparation of accounts from] incomplete records' in a not dissimilar manner, and the widespread absence of satisfactory accounting records in these early days may also have provided the motivation for such *de novo* valuations.

Capital and revenue distinction
Apart from the question of choice of an appropriate 'valuation' concept in accounting for fixed assets, other substantial difficulties faced early company director and accountants. One such difficulty, which is in fact symptomatic of the general problem presented by the double entry accounting system, concerns the need to classify *all* negative cash flows as either *asset* or *expense*. The result of such classification process is, of course, critical in terms of both the profit and loss account and the balance sheet. If, for example, a payment of cash expended to acquire a fixed asset were to be incorrectly classified as expense then the result would be to *understate* profit (revenue minus expense) for the period while similarly *understating* the value of assets. Conversely, if cash paid in the discharge of an expense were to be incorrectly classified as an asset, then the result would be to *overstate* profit for the period while similarly *overstating* the value of assets. It is this double negative or double positive effect (the propensity of the double entry model to understate or overstate *both* profits and assets simultaneously as a result of incorrect classification) which lies at the heart of much of the criticism of nineteenth-century published accounts.

Even if the line between asset and expense could be drawn with certainty, a considerable temptation for a dishonest manager to classify expenditure inappropriately would remain. A desire to inflate profits, for example, could be fulfilled by a simple recording of an expense as an asset which, as an added bonus, would also result in an equal increase in the value of assets on the balance sheet. Alternatively, a desire to deflate profits could be achieved equally simply, by recording an asset as an expense. In this case, as well as achieving the objective the 'added bonus' would be in the more covert form of a secret reserve, a physical asset in the possession of the business no trace of which would appear on the face of the balance sheet. In practice, as generations of accountants have discovered, the line between what constitutes asset and an expense defies strict definition. Hence, to a greater or lesser extent, subjective judgment must always play a part in the classification process, a circumstance which placed the managers and directors whom the reporting process was intended to control either in a moral dilemma or in a position to exploit their roles.

Periodic allocations of cost

Little distinction was drawn between capital and revenue expenditure before the advent of the double entry system. Industrialization led to increased expenditure by businesses on fixed assets and led to a search for a more sophisticated form of capital expenditure accounting. However, historians have underlined the relatively low level of fixed investment required in many business (Pollard 1963), while G.A. Lee (1975: 18) pointed to possible advantages in the old system in which 'accounting for capital expenditure on a cash flow basis would largely guarantee solvency'. As a result of this, and in the absence of any form of legislative guidance, no definitive new capital asset accounting methodology emerged. Rather, a number of policies for dealing with capital expenditure developed during the eighteenth and nineteenth centuries which at best may be described as haphazard and moreover were not consistently applied, either over time or within the same organization.

The catalysts for change between the 1830s and the 1860s were the railway companies, each necessarily incorporated by private Act of Parliament. The main characteristics of these companies were their immense size compared with their predecessors (in terms of fixed capital and share holding they were multi-million pound enterprises (*ibid*: 20)), and the complete decoupling of their management function from a large, nationwide body of lay shareholders. Without specialist knowledge or access to the books of account, the shareholders were dependent on the skill and honesty of the directors whose performance they would tend to judge by the size of the profits in relation to dividends. Without proper controls, particularly in terms of the manner in which profit was measured, the scope for abuse and fraud by the directors of such organizations was obviously immense. In this context, given the huge and unprecedented capital outlays involved in setting up such enterprises and the comparatively small traffic receipts in the early years, a realistic distinction between capital and revenue expenditure was of critical importance. Not surprisingly, company directors and shareholders did not always see eye to eye.

Following the public outcry resulting from the 'railway mania' of 1845, the Monteagle Committee, appointed by the Government in 1849, declared that 'it is impossible to overrate the importance of the strict adherence to an invariable separation between the capital and income of the railway companies' (Third Report, p. viii). The upshot of this and continued public pressure was the passage of the 1868 Regulation of Railways Act.

The most important provisions of the Act outlined the form of accounts to be published by railway companies on a half-yearly basis and filed with the Board of Trade. The Act specified no fewer than thirteen separate categories of account including a 'Receipts and Expenditure on Capital Account' and a 'General Balance Sheet'. The former statement sought to compare capital receipts with expenditures to date on fixed assets (at cost), while any balance, generally representing unspent capital, was to be carried down to the latter statement. This, in turn, showed details of current assets and liabilities, including unpaid dividends and any balance of undistributed profit to date. The two statements combined to form a more conventional balance sheet, their separation in this so-called 'double account system' serving to emphasize the distinction between capital and revenue.

In the context of fixed asset accounting another important feature of the double account system was that all repairs and renewals were to be charged to revenue, the technique generally referred to as replacement accounting. This reflects the nature of railway company fixed assets, for Lardner noted (Lardner, *Railway Economy*, p. 42 quoted in Pollins, 1956) that 'the rails of a properly laid line would last from one hundred to one hundred and fifty years'. It is hardly surprising, therefore, that separate depreciation provisions in such companies were rare (G.A. Lee 1975: 32). If made at all, they were to be included in the General Balance Sheet as 'liabilities'. Finally, the 1868 Act required that engineers' certificates be appended to the half-yearly accounts to the effect that both the 'permanent way' and 'rolling stock' had been 'maintained in good working order and repair'.

While the double accounting format was extended to other public utilities, such as gas (1871) and electricity (1882), and was 'adopted, voluntarily, by many dock and harbour, and water companies' (*ibid:* 25) no such compulsory legislative pressure was brought to bear on the registered joint stock company. Not surprisingly, therefore, substantial differences were to be found in the valuation procedures employed, both between companies and over time (Edwards 1989: 113). While diminishing, such differences were certainly still in evidence at the end of the nineteenth century.

Depreciation

As a result of the Regulation of Railways Act 1868, the system of replacement accounting adopted by the railway companies eliminated, or so it was thought, much of the need to provide for depreciation. With the passage of time, however, the drawbacks of such a system are more obvious. Even in the case of a robust or long-lived asset such as a railway track or a blast furnace, at some stage either technological change may render it obsolete or managers may decide that on economic grounds the asset should not be replaced. As a result, during the life of the asset profits will have been inflated, leading either to the payment of excessive dividends or to the overstatement of capital funds in the balance sheet. Furthermore, the question then arises: what is to become of the original cost of the asset? Under the rules of replacement accounting this would still be included in full in the balance sheet, but since the asset is exhausted it will be incapable of generating further revenues against which its cost may be written off. On the other hand, even if it was decided to replace the asset in question it is extremely unlikely that its replacement would be exactly identical, in which case what, if anything, could be done to reflect any element of 'improvement'?

With hindsight, the obvious alternative to this approach is to devise some system of allocation whereby the cost of a fixed asset can be transferred from capital to revenue over its estimated useful life. Apart from then explaining the treatment of the cost of the asset on its exhaustion this system also ensures that each accounting period will bear some proportion of the total cost incurred while, in historic cost terms at least, capital will be more realistically reflected on the balance sheet. According to Littleton (1933, quoted in Edwards 1989: 116) it was not until the second half of the nineteenth century that commentators on financial matters finally rejected the valuation approach to fixed assets in favour of cost allocation.

Undoubtedly one of the major contributions to the depreciation debate during the second half of the nineteenth century was provided by the engineer, Ewing Matheson, whose study of *The Depreciation of Factories, Mines and Industrial Undertakings, and their Valuation* was published in 1884, followed by a second edition in 1893. Matheson was one of the first writers to distinguish properly between depreciation, obsolescence and fluctuation in value (G.A. Lee 1975: 30). Matheson also urged the need for regular depreciation charges and appears to have regarded depreciation, very much in the modern mode, as a means of measurement and allocation of capital cost over time. He was also aware of the income tax implications in this respect, referring to the effects of both the Finance Act 1842 and the Customs and Inland Revenue Act 1878. For income tax purposes, the latter Act allowed reasonable depreciation of plant and machinery (although not of buildings), whereas the former had allowed only the cost of 'repairs and alterations' up to the average of the previous three years (*ibid:* 31).

The years between 1850 and 1900 represented a period of vast transition from the haphazard methods of valuation and depreciation of the early nineteenth century to a more coherent and formal allocation and matching process. This transition was neither smooth nor consistent. Brief (1965) observed that financial reports of the period are bound to be littered with inaccuracies, mistakes and non-comparable treatments which he refers to collectively as 'nineteenth century accounting error'. Edwards attributed this partly to ignorance and partly to management's determination to keep its options open regarding the level of reported profit (Edwards 1989: 116), see also Pitts (1998).

Review

The foregoing discussion has drawn attention to substantial evidence of the variety of accounting principles and practices adopted by Victorian companies, particularly in the area of fixed asset accounting. Examples of depreciation are abundant, though sometimes charged at a percentage rate and sometimes at a flat rate; applied in some years but not in others; sometimes deducted from the value of the assets in question and sometimes appropriated to a separate reserve fund. Miscellaneous credit balances, generated perhaps as a result of a capital profit or a premium on the issue of shares, were also utilized as a surrogate for depreciation to write down the book value of fixed assets. This diversity of approach presents a serious problem for researchers concerned with generalizing about capital allocation methods, depreciation, profit and dividends in the nineteenth century, and requires a powerful methodology to produce any reasonably confident conclusions. Such a methodology has been devised by the present researchers in an attempt to overcome some of the worst of these problems and is outlined in the following section.

4 METHODOLOGY

From our review of the development of corporate financial reporting to 1914 two dominant features emerge. First, the total lack of any *compulsory* accounting and auditing requirement for ordinary commercial and industrial joint stock companies between 1856 and 1900 (section 2); second, the growing reliance placed by users of company financial information during this period on some concept of *profit*, both as a yardstick for dividend payment, and as an index of management performance (section 3). They appear to be quite contradictory. On the one hand, it seems that a growing demand existed for reliable published financial reports which highlighted profitability; at the same time, a lack of statutory regulation seems to have left directors free to provide as much, or as little, information to shareholders and to the world at large as they felt to be 'beneficial'. Furthermore, since much of what is now regarded as generally accepted accounting practice, concerning for example profit measurement and asset valuation, was in a process of development during this period (see section 3), management was provided with still greater room for financial manoeuvre.

It is hardly surprising, therefore, that the tone of much of the recent academic debate relating to the reliability of financial reports during this period has been very pessimistic. For example, after examining the concept of profit in use in Britain between 1760 and 1900, G.A. Lee (1975) commented that, 'few if any series of profit figures before 1900 can be taken at their face value', while T.A. Lee (1978) characterized historians' attempts to analyse balance sheets as likely to lead to conclusions which are at best inaccurate, and at worst, 'downright misleading'. Brief (1965), Marriner (1980) and Wale (1990) emphasized the impossibility of assessing magnitudes of error contained in published accounts of the period, or even the direction in which the magnitude and the effect of such error might lie.

Probably more than any other author, Brief encapsulates the historian's dilemma in respect of nineteenth-century accounts by introducing the concept of 'accounting error'. He defines this as the failure to distinguish systematically between capital and revenue expenditures and the failure to allocate periodically the cost of fixed assets to expense (1965: 14). Such 'error', Brief concludes, is likely to result from a combination of the following factors:

1. the lack of adequate capital/ revenue distinction,
2. inadequate or non-existent depreciation policies, and
3. the widespread use of so-called secret reserves.[5]

As a potential solution to these problems the present study has sought to move away from the traditional accruals-based context, within which the accounts were originally fashioned, to a 'cash flow' basis, similar to that practised in modern day accounting under the terms of Financial Reporting Standard (FRS) No. 1. The employment of such a technique is not entirely new. Both T.A. Lee (1978) and Edwards and Webb (1982) have made use of a similar, although much more limited, methodology. In analysing the financial performance of the Distillers Company between 1830 and 1950, Lee constructed a series of four aggregated 'funds flow' statements (Statement of Standard Accounting Practice (SSAP No. 10, 1973), each covering an irregular period of between twelve and eighteen years. Similarly, Edwards and Webb's (1982) financial analysis of the Wigan Coal and Iron Company between 1865 and 1929 presented aggregated funds statements for the periods 1870–93 and 1894–1903 respectively. In contrast to these earlier works, however, our study seeks to emphasize the concept of *cash flow* rather than that of the *flow of funds*, in line with current recommended practice in corporate financial reporting (ASB, FRS 1, Revised 1996).

Perhaps more importantly, for the first time our study seeks in an extended historical analysis, to present such data on an *annualized* basis over a period of forty or fifty years rather than on an *aggregate* basis as employed by T.A. Lee (1978) and Edwards and Webb (1982).[6]

The major advantage of the cash/funds flow form of presentation is avoidance of the depreciation problem and of ironing out the effect of any valuation manipulations which have taken place (T.A. Lee 1978: 244). It would be misleading, however, to see the technique as a panacea for all the ills of nineteenth-century financial reporting. The preparation of such

---

5. The term 'secret reserve' is much used, but often ill defined, in the accounting history literature. The term is generally used to describe a credit balance of shareholders' funds, undisclosed, for some reason, on the face of a company's balance sheet. Such balance may have been created by a covert transfer from operating profit, or by directly earmarking some sundry income of the company which should, more properly, have been passed through the profit and loss account. Somewhat confusingly, however, the term is also used where expenditure of a capital nature has been written off, either overtly or covertly, against reserves, or against an undistributed profit and loss account balance. In such a situation the rather alarming end result would be for both the reserve and the asset represented by it to disappear completely from the face of the company's balance sheet.
6. The data collection and analysis phase of this project has involved four elements. Firstly, for each company examined, data as presented in surviving accounts and records were transferred to a spreadsheet. Secondly, these data were transformed to generate comparable profit and loss, balance sheet, and cash flow statements. Thirdly, individual elements of the data set are undergoing further analysis. Fourthly, further refinement of the comparable financial statements is in progress.

statements still relies heavily on the underlying annual balance sheet and profit and loss account of the organization in question. Thus, given the variety and inconsistency of accounting and reporting practices employed during the period, both between companies and over time within the same company, a first step towards the preparation of an annual cash flow statement must be the reconstruction of each published balance sheet and profit and loss account into a 'standardized' form (Baldwin, Berry and Church 1992).

A mere reshuffling of the published figures, however, would be of only limited usefulness (Napier 1989). Obviously, standardization can only be meaningful if some degree of comparability can also be introduced into the accounting policies and practices underpinning the financial reports in question. In this context the present study has attempted to identify those areas of nineteenth-century published accounts which appear to have given rise to particular criticism among earlier researchers summarized above. Wherever possible, our research has attempted to go behind the published accounts with the aid of surviving books of account and financial records. In particular, this process has sought to identify and explain movements in various key figures in annual published financial reports, notably fixed assets, share and loan capital, reserves and profit and loss account balances.

Identifying the changing constitution of these figures on an annual basis has enabled us to attempt to capture and add back capital expenditures which originally may have been written off to revenue, as well as revealing the nature and measuring the extent of depreciation charges.[7]

Standardized accounts
Voluntary disclosure
Prior to 1900, a gulf appears to have existed between what British corporate law *required* (a 'complete absence of statutory regulation in matters relating to accounting and audit' (Edey 1956: 223)) and what in practice even 'non-regulated' companies chose *voluntarily* to disclose. A set of voluntary rules relating to both accounting disclosure and audit requirement did exist during this period (see section 2). These were contained within Table B of the Joint Stock Companies Act 1856 (later to become Table A of the Companies Act 1862) and were designed to be used as a company's articles of association where the company did not file its own alternative clauses. The question must be asked therefore: to what extent were these regulations adopted and adhered to in practice?

Opinions on this topic vary widely. Quoting evidence to the 1877 Select Committee on the Companies Acts, Edey and Panitpakdi (1956: 362) have expressed some doubt as to whether many companies in fact adopted Table B or A. The source of this opinion is probably the evidence given to the Committee by David Chadwick MP, a leading accountant

---

7. The original data spreadsheets formed part of the grant report on ESRC Project 234513, and can be acquired either through the ESRC Archive, or from the authors.

and company promoter, to the effect that 'not one per cent. of the companies established [under Companies Act 1862] have adopted Schedule A'. Alternatively, Edwards (1989: 192), on the one hand, quotes from the *Accountant* (16 April 1877, p. 219) to the effect that, 'there are a very large number [of companies] registered without articles, and so entirely governed by Table A', while on the other, he contrasts this evidence with that given by the president of the ICAEW, Frederick Whinney (*Accountant,* 27 October 1888, p. 695) that very few companies adopted Table A.

Part of the reason for these seemingly conflicting views may be that Whinney had in mind the practice adopted among large, non-close companies, which tended to have articles prepared in accordance with their own special requirements; whereas, to save unnecessary expense, small companies adopted the provisions of Table A without amendment. Furthermore, Chadwick's evidence may need to be viewed with some degree of scepticism since at the time he was seeking to elicit statutory support for a set of standardized accounts which he presented to the Lowe Committee in 1877. In any event, by 1890 the model provisions were being described as 'somewhat antiquated' and 'cumbersome and almost obsolete' (*Accountant,* 6 December 1890, p. 669) and in 1895 the Davey Committee (para. 61) advocated the redrafting of Table A, 'to make it conform more closely to modern practice and business requirements.'

Such empirical work as exists in this area has been carried out by Edwards and Webb (1985). This study compares the accounting and auditing provisions contained in the articles of association of a sample of thirty companies in coal, iron and steel, and incorporated under the provisions of the Companies Act 1862, with the specimen provisions contained in Table A of that Act. They include companies of different size, from very large and influential (Consett Iron Company and Bolckow Vaughan) to the comparatively small and less significant (Sheldon Iron Steel and Coal Company and John Spencer and Sons). Of the thirty companies only one adopted Table A without amendment, effectively reducing the sample size to twenty-nine.

Perhaps the most significant finding of this study is the fact that all twenty-nine companies incorporated some form of financial reporting and auditing provision within their articles of association although, on the basis of this survey, the extent of such provision was significantly less than was envisaged by Table A of the Companies Act 1862 (Edwards and Webb: 194).

Another important issue is the extent to which clauses 79 and 80 of Table A, or some derivative thereof relating to the publication and content of the profit and loss account, were included in companies' articles of association. The view expressed in the contemporary literature reported by Edwards and Webb was that provisions relating to the profit and loss account were, 'frequently omitted or else considerably modified'. Their own research, however, confirms this view only in part, since of the companies covered in their survey 'less than a third omitted the publication requirement whereas over 80% failed to specify content' (*ibid.*). This would appear to indicate a far more significant level of disclosure in terms of profit and loss account publication than might be expected, given also the great emphasis placed upon confidentiality by business men at that time. A significant flaw in the Edwards and Webb study however is that, by the authors' own admission, the research *failed* to 'examine the relationship between companies' articles of association and actual accounting practice' (*ibid:* 177). In other words, while investigating at great length what company promoters *claimed* that management would do, the study failed completely to establish whether such mandate was actually carried out in practice.

Even casual observation shows that words and actions in this respect were sometimes very different. The articles of Henry Briggs, Son and Company, for example, a company not included in the Edwards and Webb sample but which is similar to those included, promised the production of an annual income and expenditure account, distinguishing the various sources of gross income and heads of gross expenditure very much in line with clause 80 of Table A. In the event, between 1865, when the company was incorporated, and 1900 no such statement was ever published. Rather, appended to the annual balance sheet was a directors' report setting out no more than the appropriations of net profit for the year, such as the payment of dividends and transfers to reserve, but giving no indication as to how the figure of 'profit' had been computed. This level of profit disclosure seems to represent the norm during the period under review.

Standard accounting features
From the foregoing it can be concluded that, in practice, published financial reports for the period 1862–1914 were likely to consist of some form of balance sheet, probably subject to a degree of external audit, together with a directors' report. Balance sheets were generally presented in the traditional double-sided 'English' form (Edey and Panitpakdi 1956: 366): 'capital and liabilities' appearing on the left hand side and 'property and assets' on the right. Unconstrained by today's statutory regulation as to content and form, the directors' report generally presented a review of trading conditions and financial results for the period, together with recommendations as to the appropriation of profit.

Perhaps the first important general observation to make concerning the use of nineteenth-century accounts is that the balance sheet in a given year was a penultimate rather than a final statement. Each year's balance sheet contained a statement of net profit earned, generally in the form of a single figure without explanation as to its computation. The annexed directors' report contained recommendations about the appropriation of profit, for example, the establishment or augmenting of a reserve or the payment of dividends. These recommendations were agreed at the company's annual general meeting, took effect, and were incorporated into the balance sheet of the following year.

The second point which deserves comment is that the classification and grouping of items in nineteenth-century accounts were unlike those in accounts of today. On the 'liabilities side' of the balance sheet, for example, it is often difficult to distinguish between long-term and short-term debt. This is quite surprising, given the generally accepted view (Yamey, Edwards) that the 'double account' ethos prevailed at that time, in which the preference was for share capital and long-term debt to be represented by long-term investment in capital assets. Similarly, on the 'assets side' the line between fixed and current items in nineteenth-century accounts was often drawn in an unfamiliar way. A good example of this can be seen from the pro-forma balance sheet attached to Table A of the Companies Act 1862. Here a distinction was drawn, not between fixed and current assets, but between 'movable' and 'immovable' property (see section 2), thus, 'plant' was classified with 'stock in trade', rather than, as would now more generally be the case, with 'land and buildings'.

A copy of the pro-forma profit and loss account and balance sheet used for the purpose of the present study is shown in Table 4.1 at the end of this section. For ease of transfer into a spreadsheet format both statements are presented in the more modern, 'vertical' form. Wherever possible, however, every attempt was made to retain the 'richness' of the original data set, particularly where the information available was likely to have a measurable effect on cash flow. Hence, for example, the retention of a heading for 'calls in advance' (i.e. cash prepaid to the company by shareholders for the purchase of shares) in the pro-forma balance sheet.

The pro-forma profit and loss account is, in effect, little more than an 'appropriation' account. Figures relating to costs and revenues were generally found to be in very short supply among the sample companies. More often than not, however, a statement of 'profit' for the year (either before or after depreciation) was given, sometimes as part of the directors' report or as part of the balance sheet. The standardized format begins, therefore, with the profit figure before depreciation and proceeds to deduct depreciation (where known or deducible from elsewhere) and 'special expenditure'. This term was that generally applied by the researchers to describe capital expenditure on fixed assets which had, for one reason or another, been charged directly against profit or reserves. In other words, such spends were treated as being in the nature of either a surrogate for, or an addition to, the annual depreciation charge. Dividends and transfers to reserves were then deducted, including, as outlined above, proposals for such detailed in the directors' report. The balance of unappropriated profit was finally added to reserves brought forward from previous years and the total included in the pro-forma balance sheet.

The form of the balance sheet is essentially conventional. The specific nature of most of the items included therein is described in a detailed example below. One or two points are, however, worthy of special mention at this stage. The share capital section of the balance sheet includes a separate heading for 'share premium'. This refers to amounts which shareholders have been required to pay to the company over and above the face value of the shares which they were seeking to purchase. Obviously such amounts have a direct relationship to cash inflow and are thus of particular importance in the context of the current research. Similarly, where possible, movements in fixed assets were broken down so as to reveal cash outflows and inflows in relation to additions and disposals thereof. 'Special expenditures' were included in the value of such additions and subsequently deducted as part of the charge for depreciation, as described above. The note at the foot of the pro-forma balance sheet (Table 4.1) outlines the mechanics of this process.

Cash flow statements
Profit and cash flow
In the past, business historians have often made use of surviving company profit and loss accounts and balance sheets. However, significantly less use has been made of data reflecting the underlying cash flows. This is perhaps not surprising, given the complexity of the profit/cash relationship. The links between traditional accounting reports and cash flows, previously introduced in section 3, are now demonstrated in greater detail using a simplified example outlined below.

The balance sheet of company, A Limited, appears (in vertical form) on 1 January 20xx as follows:

BALANCE SHEET as at 1 January 20xx

		£
SHAREHOLDERS EQUITY		
	Share capital	50
	Reserves:	
	Profit and loss account balance	11
		61
FIXED ASSETS		
	Plant and machinery	40
CURRENT ASSETS		
	Stock	10
	Trade debtors	8
	Cash in hand	12
		30
CURRENT LIABILITIES		
	Trade creditors	(6)
	Proposed dividend	(3)
		21
		61

During the twelve months to 31 December 20xx, various cash transactions took place, summarized as follows:

CASH TRANSACTION SUMMARY
for the year ended 31 December 20xx

	£
CASH RECEIPTS	
Trade debtors	127
CASH PAYMENTS	
Trade creditors	(65)
Overhead costs	(24)
Additional plant and machinery	(18)
Dividends paid	(13)
Cash surplus for the year	7
Cash in hand 1 January 20xx	12
Cash in hand 31 December 20xx	19

As previously outlined in section 3, the above cash receipts and payments provide the 'raw material' from which traditional accounting reports (the profit and loss account and balance sheet) are derived. However, the transformation process is complex. Not only does it seek to integrate the cash flows with the opening financial position illustrated by the above balance sheet, but also with similar 'closing' data (at 31 December 20xx in this case). Decisions as to the company's accounting policy in relation to such matters as depreciation and bad debts must also be considered.

For the purposes of the present example this additional 'closing' information is summarized as follows:

CLOSING INFORMATION as at 31 December 20xx

	£
Stock	14
Trade debtors	13
Trade creditors	9

A final dividend of 10% is proposed.
Depreciation is charged at 20% per annum on the value of fixed assets.
Bad debts and taxation are ignored.

With the data set now available it is possible to prepare a profit and loss account for A Limited for the year ended 31 December 20xx, as well as a balance sheet at that date. Such statements (in vertical form) might appear as follows:

PROFIT AND LOSS ACCOUNT
for the year ended 31 December 20xx

	Notes	£
Sales revenue	a	132
Cost of sales	b	(64)
		68
Overhead costs	c	(36)
		32
Dividends	d	(15)
Retained profit	e	17

BALANCE SHEET as at 31 December 20xx

	Notes	£
SHAREHOLDERS EQUITY		
Share capital	f	50
Reserves:		
Profit and loss account balance	g	28
		78
FIXED ASSETS	h	
Plant and machinery		46
CURRENT ASSETS	i	
Stock		14
Trade debtors		13
Cash in hand		19
		46
CURRENT LIABILITIES	j	
Trade creditors		(9)
Proposed dividend		(5)
		32
		78

Even in this very simple example, a cursory inspection of the above financial reports is sufficient to reveal that the figures included therein are very far removed from their cash flow origins. For example, the £17 'retained profit' for the year does not equate, even closely, with the £7 'cash surplus' derived from the cash transaction summary. The uninitiated may feel, quite reasonably, that it should! Similarly, the figures of 'revenue' and 'costs' included in the profit and loss account are difficult to link to their cash flow counterparts. Before proceeding further, therefore, some explanation of the derivation of these figures is required, beginning with the profit and loss account.

In essence, a profit and loss account seeks to *match* the sales output ('revenue'/'turnover') of an organization for a given period of time (commonly one year) with the resources consumed ('costs'/'expenses') in generating that output. Clearly, the conceptual problems involved in this 'resource matching' process are of a totally different order to those encountered in the simple measurement of cash inflows and outflows. Thus, taking the headings from the above profit and loss account in turn:

a. 'Sales revenue' records the value of goods or services sold by the company during the year. However, not all sales will have been for cash. Indeed, in this example, it has been assumed that *all* sales have involved the exchange of goods or services for a *promise* to pay. Those individuals and companies who made these promises have thus become the company's 'trade debtors'. The amounts owed feature in the balance sheets as a current asset, until the promises to pay are redeemed with cash. Thus, the trade debtor figure of £8 appearing in the opening balance sheet (representing cash receivable from a sale in the *previous* year) forms a part of the £127 cash received from debtors in the *current* year. Conversely, the closing trade debtor figure of £13, while representing a sale of goods in the *current* year, will not manifest itself in cash flow terms until received from the debtor during the year following. The figure of 'sales revenue' in the profit and loss account (the value of goods or services physically sold during the year) is, therefore, computed as: cash received from trade debtors during the year, less value of opening trade debtors, plus value of closing trade debtors = (£127 - £8 + £13) = £132.

b. 'Cost of sales' are those expenses directly incurred in generating the sales turnover. The nature of such costs depends on the type of business in question. In a manufacturing context, for example, costs will include not only raw materials, but also the cost of labour and other resources involved in converting those materials into units of finished product. However, some raw materials and labour may have been acquired during the accounting period in exchange for a promise to pay.

Again, in this example, it has been assumed that *all* such acquisitions have involved the exchange of goods or services for a *promise* to pay. Those individuals and companies who have received these promises have become the company's 'trade creditors'. The amounts owed feature in the balance sheets as a current liability until the promises to pay are redeemed with cash. Thus, just as with the 'sale of goods', illustrated above, the figure of raw materials and labour acquired is computed as: cash paid to trade creditors during the year, less value of opening trade creditors, plus value of closing trade creditors = (£65 - £6 + £9) = £68.

It will be noted at this point, however, that the figure of £68 still does <u>not</u> correspond with the figure of 'cost of sales' appearing in the profit and loss account. This is because more, or less, resource may have been used to generate the turnover than was actually acquired during the year. The difference is explained by any decrease/(increase) over time in the value of 'stock' appearing in the company's balance sheet. Thus, in the present example, a 'stock adjustment' of £-(4) (opening stock £10, less closing stock £14) must be *deducted* from the cost of raw materials and labour acquired, since this cost is <u>not</u> associated with the generation of the current year's sales revenue but with an increase in the company's stock holding. 'Cost of sales' is, therefore, computed as: cost of raw materials and labour acquired +/- stock adjustment = (£68 - £4) = £64.

c. 'Overhead costs' comprise other costs associated with the company's activities, but not directly related to manufacturing or trading. Again, however, this is not necessarily a record of expenses paid in cash. These are amounts which must be paid sooner or later as a consequence of the consumption of resources during the accounting period. If some part has not yet been paid it will feature in the balance sheet as a general creditor: a further current liability.

While the costs of £24 paid in cash in the present example are assumed for the sake of simplicity to relate entirely to resources consumed in the current year, 'depreciation' may also feature as a cost in this context. It represents an allowance for the fact that use will have reduced the utility of the company's fixed asset base, its plant and machinery in this case, although no direct cash outflow from the company in this respect will have occurred. Cash changes hands only when fixed assets are acquired or disposed of rather than when depreciation is charged.

The accounting policy of the company in this example is assumed to be to charge depreciation at 20% per annum on the 'net book value' of its fixed assets, the so-called 'reducing balance' method. Thus, an opening fixed asset balance of £40 is augmented by expenditure of £18 during the year to give a total net book value of £58. Depreciation at 20% thereon equals (approximately) £12. 'Overhead costs' are therefore computed in this case as indirect costs paid in cash plus depreciation = (£24 + £12) = £36.

d. 'Dividends' represent the proportion of profit due to the shareholders. They will eventually manifest themselves as cash in the hands of shareholders, a clear flow of cash *out* of the company. However, the dividends may or may not have been paid out by the company during the accounting period. Any dividend proposed but unpaid at the accounting date will feature in the balance sheet as a current liability.

In the present example the proposed dividend of £3 appearing in the opening balance sheet forms part of the dividend payment of £13 made by the company during the year. The remaining £10 represents an 'interim' dividend (declared and paid) during the current year. At the end of the year, based on its trading results, the company proposes the payment of a further 10% of its issued share capital as a 'final' dividend. Thus, the dividend charge appearing in the profit and loss account represents the sum of the current year's dividends (irrespective of the date of payment); that is, the interim dividend paid, plus the final dividend (10% x £50) proposed = (£10 + £5) = £15.

e. 'Retained profit' is that portion of the annual profit *not* distributed by the company to its shareholders. It will appear ultimately as an addition to 'shareholders' equity' in the closing balance sheet. It should be clear from the preceding discussion, however, that profit is not a cash-based concept. There is, therefore, no suggestion that the retained profit figure in the profit and loss account in any way represents a store of cash held in the company.

We turn now to an analysis of the balance sheet. A balance sheet seeks to present a picture of the financial position of an organization at a given point in time, usually at the end of an accounting period for which a profit and loss account has been prepared. 'Financial position' in this context is an extremely hybrid notion, underpinned by the principles of double-entry bookkeeping, which seeks to compare the future financial benefits (assets) of an organization with its future financial commitments (liabilities). The net of these two gives a measure of the capital investment of the owners (shareholders 'funds'/'equity'). Taking the headings from the above balance sheet in turn:

    f. 'Share capital' represents an accumulation of the cash supplied to the company by its shareholders in exchange for the issue of shares throughout the life of the company. The increase/(decrease) in this item between successive balance sheets normally represents a cash flow into/(from) the company during an accounting period. On occasions, however, a free 'bonus' or 'scrip' issue of shares may take place. This will normally have been 'financed' by a transfer from reserves, or perhaps by a revaluation of fixed assets. In either case, it is important to note that although the structure of the balance sheet may change profoundly following such a transaction, no *cash* will have changed hands. For simplicity, the present example assumes no change in share capital during the year.

    g. 'Reserves' represent an accumulation of profits retained, period by period, over the life of the company. Together with share capital they give a measure of the total investment (funds/equity) made over time by shareholders and represented in physical terms by the company's total net assets. Reserves may be specifically labelled: for example, 'revenue reserve', or 'general reserve'. In the present example the label 'profit and loss account balance' denotes an accumulation of past unappropriated profits, as indicated in the opening balance sheet, with those of the current year = (£11 + £17) = £28.

    h. 'Fixed assets' represent one of the more complex balance sheet items. It is an accumulation of capital investment expenditures over the life of the company. However, the accounting process also recognizes that fixed assets are being consumed, over time, by the act of production and trading. Thus the depreciation item (as previously outlined in note c above) seeks to measure and adjust for this reduction in the utility of the company's fixed asset base. Assuming, for the sake of simplicity, no sale of assets during an accounting period, then the change in fixed assets between successive balance sheets is measured by:

Fixed assetsBS(t-1) + Investment - DepreciationPL = Fixed assetsBS(t), which in the present example = (£40 + £18 - £12) = £46.

Note that the *cash* movement, effectively *hidden* in this relationship, is the cash outflow on new fixed asset investment of £18

    i. 'Current assets' are held by a company as a consequence of the production and trading process. They represent stages in the transformation of cash into raw materials, finished goods, into debtors, and finally back into cash. The existence of such assets on the balance sheet indicates that cash has been used (or will be used) to acquire them. Assuming current liabilities remain constant, the amount of cash which has been used in the current time period is given by the difference between the figures in two successive balance sheets. For example, if [Stock(t) - Stock(t-1)] > 0, then cash has been used to build up stock. If [Stock(t) - Stock(t-1)] < 0 then the run-down of stock will have released cash for use elsewhere in the company. This is an important relationship to which we will return later.

The current asset 'cash in hand' requires further individual comment. The figure represents a 'stock' of cash held to support the company's activities. In part, its level will be determined by the scale of activity of the company: the more bills to be paid the more cash the company needs to keep at hand. The cash element in the balance sheet represents an investment decision as much as does the fixed asset element. The amount of cash flow used, or released during the accounting period, is shown by the difference between the 'cash in hand' amounts appearing in successive balance sheets.

j. 'Current liabilities' represent amounts of cash which the company must pay out during the next accounting period. The amount of cash actually paid, for example in dividends, during the accounting period (t-1) to t may be derived by:

$$\text{Div BS(t-1)} + \text{DivPL} - \text{DivBS(t)} = \text{Div Cash Flow}$$

where BS and PL indicate balance sheet and profit and loss account elements respectively. This is a simple representation of the fundamental accounting identity: Opening balance + Inflow - Outflow = Closing balance.

Cash flow statements

While 'profitability' remains an important factor in the measurement of corporate performance, the second half of the twentieth century witnessed a growing disquiet among users with the quality of reported accounting information. In particular, the validity of the process of 'accounting allocation' (T.A. Lee 1984), demonstrated above in respect of debtors, creditors, stock and depreciation, has increasingly been called into question. The search for reliable and objective alternatives, however, has proved less than successful. Perhaps the greatest innovation in recent years has been the wider recognition of the importance of *liquidity* (cash flow) to an organization's survival and growth. The requirement for UK companies to publish a 'cash flow statement' as part of their annual financial report and accounts (ASB, FRS 1, Revised 1996) represents a major step forward.

In the USA the origins of such statement can be traced back still further to the publication of Opinion No. 3, *The Statement of Source and*

Application of Funds (1963) by the US Accounting Principles Board.[8] By 1970 such statement was a compulsory part of corporate financial reporting in the USA. In the UK, however, even by the early 1970s, the funds/cash flow statement was still considered somewhat *avant-garde*. For example, G.A. Lee's *Modern Financial Accounting* (1973), a standard professional text of the time, devotes only some six pages (of 614) to this topic. 'Before leaving the subject of accounting reform', Lee writes, 'it is convenient to examine briefly a topic which has received a good deal of attention in recent years, though its principles have been known much longer—namely, the measurement of an entity's *flow of funds* over a year or other period. Connected with this is the subordinate *flow of cash* over the same period.'

The first widespread application of the funds/cash flow technique in the UK, followed publication of SSAP 10, *Statements of Source and Application of Funds* (1975) by the Accounting Standards Steering Committee. In line with the earlier American model the proposed statement was couched in terms of 'funds' rather than cash, although the precise meaning of this term was not defined by the statement! Throughout the following decade various moves for the refinement and extension of the technique were advanced. T.A. Lee (1984), for example, advocated 'a unified system of cash flow reporting', which moved away completely from the traditional emphasis on the historic cost profit measurement model.

In September 1991 the newly formed UK Accounting Standards Board produced, as its first financial reporting standard, FRS 1, *Cash Flow Statements*. The standard included an explanation and justification of the proposed move from a funds flow to cash flow reporting (para. 51). Furthermore, and perhaps most significantly, the FRS 1 format, like the Lee model before it, had at its very foundation the presentation of a figure of so-called 'cash flow from operating activities': a representation in cash flow rather than 'profit' terms of the results of matching current period 'sales revenues' with 'costs'. Such a figure, which is free from the subjective influences of accounting valuation and allocations, represents a more meaningful measure of corporate performance than its more common 'accruals based' counterpart (T.A. Lee 1984). In 1996 the suggested format of the FRS 1 cash flow statement was revised but its general thrust remained unaltered.

In essence, the technique for reporting cash flows in this manner relies on the comparison of information contained in the traditional historic cost balance sheets at the beginning and end of an accounting period. Marginal changes in the various classes of asset and liability between these two dates are construed as representing some measure of cash inflows and outflows for the intervening period as follows:

---

8. The somewhat esoteric concept of 'funds flow' (seeking to classify balance sheet movements in terms of changes in working capital) as opposed to 'cash flow', is unimportant in the current context. Indeed, subsequent accounting standards on both sides of the Atlantic have moved significantly in favour of the latter form.

Figure 4.1

	CASH INFLOWS	CASH OUTFLOWS
REPRESENTED BY	+ capital/liabilities − assets	+ assets − capital/liabilities

To the non-accountant, the concept of an increase in liabilities equating with an increase in cash may seem puzzling. Reference back to the double entry model shown in Figure 3.1 and the accompanying explanation may help to clarify this. In effect, all that the cash flow calculus seeks to do, in the absence of the original cash transaction data, is to work *backwards* from the published financial reports to some, all be it highly aggregated, measure of the cash flows underpinning them.

The addition of profit and loss account information for the intervening period allows the calculus to proceed one stage further. Since we have shown that neither sales revenue nor costs are exclusively cash-based concepts, profit is clearly not a good guide to the net cash flow of a company for a given period. Adjustments have to be made. The non-cash, depreciation element in costs must be added back to profit, and allowance made for marginal changes in stock, debtors, and creditors between the opening and closing balance sheets.

The following illustrates the method of deriving a 'cash flow statement' using the accounts of A Limited prepared in the previous section. Firstly, the balance sheets of that company as at 1 January 20xx and 31 December 20xx appeared as follows:

BALANCE SHEETS as at 1 January 20xx and 31 December 20xx

	£ 1 Jan.	£ 31 Dec.
SHAREHOLDERS EQUITY		
Share capital	50	50
Reserves:		
Profit and loss account balance	11	28
	61	78
FIXED ASSETS		
Plant and machinery	40	46
CURRENT ASSETS		
Stock	10	14
Trade debtors	8	13
Cash in hand	12	19
	30	46
CURRENT LIABILITIES		
Trade creditors	(6)	(9)
Proposed dividend	(3)	(5)
	21	32
	61	78

By comparing these two balance sheets, in the manner outlined in Figure 4.1 (see page 36), valuable preliminary data is provided as to the nature of the intervening cash flows:

PRELIMINARY CASH FLOW STATEMENT
for the year ended 31 December 20xx

	Notes	£	
CASH INFLOWS			
= (+ capital/ liabilities) or (- assets)			
Profit and loss account balance	a	17	(28 -11)
Trade creditors		3	(9 - 6)
Proposed dividend	b	2	(5 - 3)
		22	
CASH OUTFLOWS			
= (+assets) or (- capital/ liabilities)			
Plant and Machinery	c	(6)	(46 - 40)
Stock		(4)	(14 - 10)
Debtors		(5)	(13 - 8)
Increase in cash in hand		7	(19 - 12)

In this form the statement provides a very incomplete guide to A Limited's cash flows for the year ended 31 December 20xx; this is indicated by a comparison with the cash transaction summary appearing at the beginning of the example. However, we have outlined how by referring to the profit and loss account for the intervening period, the statement can become more complete.

a. The above 'profit and loss account balance' figure of £17 represents profit *after* depreciation (a non-cash flow cost) and also *after* dividend commitments which, it could be argued, are an *allocation* or sharing of profit rather than a cost. These two items are, therefore, 'added back' in order to provide a closer, although as yet still incomplete, measure of cash flow from the company's manufacturing and trading ('operating') activities. Thus, 'operating profit before depreciation' = (£17 + £15 + £12) = £44.

b. The net 'proposed dividend' figure of £2 does *not* represent a cash flow in the current year. Rather, the cash flow in respect of dividends for any year, as indicated in j above (page 34), is given by the total charge in the profit and loss account plus the proposed dividend figure in the opening balance sheet less the proposed dividend figure in the closing balance sheet. Thus, 'dividends paid' = (£15 + 3 - £5) = £13.

c. Like the 'profit' figure, referred to in a above, the cash outflow on 'plant and machinery' of £6 is currently stated *after* depreciation – a non-cash flow charge. Again, therefore, it is necessary to 'add back' the depreciation figure in order to reflect more accurately cash expended during the year on the acquisition of fixed assets. Thus 'additions to plant and machinery' = (£6 + £12) = £18.

The cash flow statement, thus revised, will now read:

REVISED CASH FLOW STATEMENT
for the year ended 31 December 20xx

	£
CASH INFLOWS	
Operating profit before depreciation	44
Trade creditors	3
	47
CASH OUTFLOWS	
Dividends paid	(13)
Plant and Machinery	(18)
Stock	(4)
Debtors	(5)
Increase in cash in hand	7

Comparison of the revised cash flow statement with the cash transaction summary listed at the start of this example is now more revealing. The figures for additions to plant and machinery, and for dividends paid are identical. Other figures still appear to be at odds but, interestingly, the *net difference* between the remaining cash inflows and outflows in each statement is the same.

CASH TRANSACTION SUMMARY

	£
REMAINING CASH RECEIPTS	
Trade debtors	127
REMAINING CASH PAYMENTS	
Trade creditors	(65)
Overhead costs	(24)
Cash surplus	38

REVISED CASH FLOW STATEMENT

	£
REMAINING CASH INFLOWS	
Profit and loss account balance	44
Trade creditors	3
	47
REMAINING CASH OUTFLOWS	
Stock	(4)
Debtors	(5)
Cash surplus	38

In each case the figure of £38, referred to above simply as 'cash surplus', is, in fact, the *cash flow from operating activities*. It is a measure of the *net cash* generated as a result of manufacturing and trading, disregarding all other possible cash inflows and outflows from, for example, share and loan transactions, or fixed asset acquisitions and sales. To the non-accountant perhaps it might best be described as a cash surrogate of the accounting concept of 'profit'.

Having once computed cash inflows and outflows in this way, the form of presentation of the cash flow statement becomes a matter of individual choice, dependent upon the emphasis required. Table 4.2 at the end of this section presents the pro-forma cash flow statement derived for the purposes of the current research. The format is similar to that recommended by FRS 1 (Revised 1996) except in the following important respects.

The profit figure, which is subjected to adjustment in this case, is profit before the deduction of depreciation and interest payments but *after* the deduction of taxation.[9] Adjustment for the changes in stock, debtors, and creditors over the period gives cash flow from operations. This is the net cash flow which running the company has made available for wider use.

Next, the deduction of 'investment' in cash is shown together with investment in fixed assets. This treatment is designed to emphasize the fact that cash flow from operations is used up by holding a cash balance, for example in a bank account, as well as by purchasing fixed assets. The cash flow remaining after these deductions is known as 'free cash flow'. It is the cash flow left after all the company's internal needs have been satisfied.

How is any remaining cash flow to be used? It is paid out as interest and dividends. If free cash flow is inadequate to support these interest and dividend cash outflows it must be augmented by a cash inflow from outside the company. Thus, free cash flow has to be equal to any new equity and debt raised less any payment of interest and dividends to shareholders.[10] Free cash flow is the same as net cash flow to shareholders and debt holders. If free cash flow is negative, then new equity and/or debt must be raised in order to meet the shortfall.

---

9. While in a present-day context, where very significant rates of corporate taxation prevail, this failure to capture separately the impact of taxation on profits and cash flows would be a serious omission, the very low tax rates in operation throughout the period under review are likely to render this issue immaterial.

10. Archival research has produced quite reliable figures in respect of the payment of dividends, however, information concerning the payments of interest is more problematic. Where the amounts of interest paid were not clear from the accounts and supporting archival records, annual estimates have been made by applying a known, or in some cases estimated, rate of interest to the average loan outstanding during the year in question: i.e. ½ (opening loan + closing loan) × interest rate.

Table 4.1. Standardised accounts pro-forma

PROFIT & LOSS ACCOUNT

Profit before depreciation
less: Depreciation
    Special expenditure*
Profit after depreciation
less: Dividends paid
    Dividends proposed
    Transfers to reserves
Unappropriated profit
add: P/L Balance b/fwd
Balance c/fwd

BALANCE SHEET

Share capital
 Ordinary shares
 Preference shares
 Calls in advance
 Share premium
Reserves
 General
 P/L Account balance
Mortgages & debentures
Fixed assets
 Tangible (see note below)
 Intangible
Current assets
 Stock
 Debtors
 Cash
Current liabilities
 Creditors & bills
 Dividends proposed
 Bank overdraft

Note:
Tangible fixed assets:
Balance b/fwd
 Additions/(disposals)
 Depreciation
 Special expenditure*
Balance c/fwd

* 'Special expenditure' is a term generally applied by the researchers to describe the charging of capital spends on fixed assets against profit or reserves.

Table 4.2. Cash flow statement pro-forma

CASH FLOW STATEMENT
Profit before depreciation and interest
    Investment in:
      Stock
      Debtors
      Creditors
Cash flow from operations
    Investment in:
      Cash & bank
      Fixed assets
Free cash flow
Cash from shareholders
    Ordinary share capital
    Dividends paid
Cash from lenders
    Issue/repayment of loans
    Interest paid
Externally generated funds

5 THE DATA SET

The second part of this monograph which follows on page 53 contains annual cash flow statements for a series of twenty companies (primarily producing coal but several also producing iron and steel) from the date of their respective incorporations (or as soon thereafter as data is available) to 1914. The sample of companies listed has not been the the result of statistically 'scientific' selection though their selection has not been random. The criteria employed in constructing the sample were as follows:

(a)   that the company produced coal;
(b)   that companies of various sizes should be included;
(c)   that a lengthy historical series of complete, or almost complete, balance sheets were available;
(d)   that either published histories or supporting archival material existed.

An index of companies so selected is provided on page 53.

Interpreting the data tables
Bell Brothers 1877
This section describes briefly the arithmetic underlying the data tables using various entries for Bell Brothers Limited. (pp. 54–58). Consider first the year 1877. The 1877 profit figure is £37,276. This is generated by the trading activities of Bell Brothers. Costs have been subtracted from sales revenue. Costs here do not include the non-cash cost of depreciation. In effect the first step has been taken in moving from the accounting profit measure to a cash flow measure; the non-cash expense of depreciation has been added back to the traditional profit measure.

The next component of the table looks at the cash flow consequences of movements in stock, debtors and creditors. The stock figure for 1877 is negative -£27,604. This indicates that the level of stock has fallen between the 1876 year end and the 1877 year end. This means that some of the costs normally deducted in the calculation of accounting profit have turned out not to involve a cash outflow. These costs represent the use of stock already held in the company. Another way of looking at this is to imagine that Bell Brothers have decided that they need less stock in order to run the business. Cash which would have been used to purchase stock is no longer needed for that purpose. There is then a reduced claim on cash flow for investment in stock. The same type of argument holds for debtors. The figure of -£5,729 indicates that debtors have fallen between the 1876 and 1877 year ends. Bell Brothers have collected cash from people who owed money to the company. In general negative figures in the stock and debtors rows of the data tables represent 'good news' in the context of cash flow generation.

1877 shows a figure of £51,056 for creditors. *The positive figure represents a reduction in creditors.* As has been said creditors represent promises to pay, so Bell Brothers have decreased the amount of their promises to pay over the year. Effectively suppliers have reduced Bell Brothers' short-term borrowing by £51,056 over the year. This reduction in borrowing power means that cash which has come into the business from trading activity has had to be used to make purchases. In general then the positive figure in the creditor row of the data tables represents 'bad news' in the context of cash flow generation.

In summary then the operations of the company have generated a cash flow of:

		£
Profit before interest and depreciation		37,276
Less:	Stock decrease	-(27,604)
	Debtor decrease	-(5,729)
	Creditor decrease	51,056
Equals: Cash flow from operations		19,553

Note that the deduction of a negative figure from profit is the mathematical equivalent of an *addition* to the total. Thus, in the data tables, when stock, debtors and creditors are being considered, negative numbers are 'good news' and positive numbers are 'bad news' in the context of cash flow generation.

What does the £19,553 of cash flow from operations mean? Imagine that there are only three entrances to the Bell Brothers mining operation. Through one entrance, Gate 1, pass all workers, raw materials, finished goods, and the cash paid and received for them. Through Gate 2 pass shareholders, lenders and taxmen, and all the cash they provide (new equity, debt), and all the cash they extract (repayment of equity and debt, dividends, interest and tax). In 1877 £19,553 more came in through Gate 1 than went out through Gate 1. The algebra and arithmetic was necessary because we did not have an observer stationed at Gate 1 counting cash in and cash out. It is that net amount which is meant by the phrase 'cash flow from operations'.

Of course, the operating cash flow figure presented here is not as pure as one might like. Taxmen have been using Gate 1, rather than Gate 2, so that 'cash flow from operations' is operating cash flow *after* taxation.

The £19,553 has work to do. Bell Brothers have chosen to increase the amount of cash they hold by £6,241, and their fixed assets by £677. It is the cash flow from operations which allows Bell Brothers to do this. The positive figures in the cash and bank and fixed asset columns represent increases during the year. They represent uses of cash. The build-up of cash and the build-up of fixed assets are both investments. (The third entrance to the Bell Brothers' operation, Gate 3, ignored so far, is needed for investment goods, workers involved in construction of new assets, and the associated cash payments. Bank deposits also pass through here.)

After making their investment decisions Bell Brothers have £12,635 remaining of their cash flow from operations. This is free cash flow. There are no further requirements within the firm to be met. This cash flow must therefore go outside the firm. It could be used to retire equity in some circumstances, or pay dividends, but as can be seen in 1877 there are zeros in these two rows in the data tables. Where did the cash go? It was used to pay interest of £12,569, and to make a net repayment of loans of £66.

The structure of the data tables should now be clearer. The first section shows the components of free cash flow, that cash flow which is left after all of the business's internal needs have been met. The second section of the tables follows this cash into the outside world of shareholders and lenders.

Bell Brothers 1887
It is useful to work through the tables for another year, 1887, since it shows a very different free cash flow situation. At first sight 1887 seems to show an improvement over 1877: profit is larger at £38,971. However, stocks and debtors have both risen, using up cash flow. The movement in creditors is also bad for cash flow. The positive entry represents a reduction in creditors, a fall in the amount of short-term loan finance suppliers are willing to allow Bell Brothers. As a result of these working capital movements cash flow from operations is £6,712, roughly one third of the 1877 figure. The potential for movements in stock, debtors and creditors to change the cash flow from operations picture should now be clear.

Despite the fact that cash flow from operations is only £6,712 Bell Brothers have invested £15,848 in fixed assets. The shortfall in cash flow has been reduced but not eliminated by running down the level of cash held at the bank. There is a negative free cash flow of £1,534, a shortfall which must be met in some way.

As can be seen, free cash flow can be negative as well as positive. If it is positive then it must flow out of the firm, either to shareholders as dividends or retirement of equity, or to lenders as interest or the repayment of debt. If free cash flow is negative, as it is in 1887, then the business has internal needs which its cash flow from operations cannot satisfy. Cash must flow into the firm to make up the shortfall. This cash can come from new equity or new debt. In this case no new equity is raised; £5,718 of additional debt meets the shortfall. It appears that too much debt has been raised, but this is not the case. Exactly enough has been raised to cover the negative free cash flow and pay interest on existing debt. Interest must be paid, even if free cash flow is insufficient. In these circumstances a company must raise new equity or debt to meet its obligations to existing shareholders or lenders.

Bell Brothers 1894
The year 1894 exhibits further interesting features. Cash flow from operations is positive at £26,919. Profit has been augmented by a reduction in stock, and on this occasion by an increase in creditors. (Remember, in this section of the data tables negative numbers are 'good news' for cash flow.) Unfortunately, there has also been a build-up of debtors. Sales have not been for cash, and therefore £46,960 must be subtracted when calculating cash flow from operations.

Bell Brothers have increased both the amount of fixed assets and their holdings of cash. The increase in the cash balance is four times the addition to fixed assets on this occasion. The build-up of cash might have come about for several reasons. It might be in anticipation of a future transaction or set of transactions, it might be a precaution against potential disruption of future cash inflows, or it might be speculative, allowing Bell Brothers to act quickly should an investment opportunity arise. It could of course be involuntary, with some anticipated payment need having failed to arise. Whatever the reason, it happened, and in conjunction with expenditure on investment on fixed assets it has reduced free cash flow to £2,386.

The free cash flow is insufficient to meet the required interest payment, and as in 1887 new debt covers the shortfall. As in 1887 more debt has been raised than appears to be necessary. On this occasion the aim is to enable Bell Brothers to pay a dividend.

The idea that paying a dividend is a necessity, not an option, is common in the finance literature. Shareholders are thought to be unhappy if dividends fall below previously achieved levels. In this view some non-discretionary dividend payment needs to be met before the phrase 'free cash flow' has any real meaning. However, this is not the view taken in the data tables. Free cash flow is the difference between cash flow from operations and uses of cash within the firm. Free cash flow in this sense is always exactly matched by externally generated funds. That is to say the two figures are equal in absolute terms but opposite in sign. However, the figure for externally generated funds is a net figure: new equity plus new debt less dividends and interest. In 1894 new debt of £12,013, less dividends paid of £6,048 and interest paid of £8,351 gives externally generated funds of -£2,386, exactly offsetting the free cash flow of £2,386.

Finally, there are one or two items in the data section for other companies which deserve particular comment:

(a) *Butterley Company Ltd:*
The table shows zero elements for the year 1889. The company was a partnership until September of that year. The year 1888 represents the final eighteen months of the partnership, ending September 1888. The data for the year 1890 covers the first eighteen months after incorporation, ending March 1890.

(b) *North's Navigation(1889) Collieries Ltd:*
The table shows zero elements for the year 1893. No accounting records were found for this year.

(c) *Pearson Knowles Coal and Iron Company Ltd:*
The cash flow is calculated from unconsolidated accounts up to 1910, and from 1911 to 1914 from consolidated figures.

REFERENCES

Accounting Standards Board (ASB) (1996), *Cash flow statements*, Financial Reporting Standard No. 1 (Revised 1996).

Accounting Standards Steering Committee (ASSC) (1975), *Statements of Source and Application of Funds*, Statement of Standard Accounting Practice No. 10.

Arnold, A.J. (1995), 'Should Historians Trust Late Nineteenth-Century Company Financial Statements?', *Business History*, Vol. 38, No. 2, pp. 40–54.

Baldwin, T.J., Berry, R.H. and Church, R.A. (1992), 'An examination of the accounts of the Consett Iron Company Limited, 1864–1914', *Accounting and Business Research*, Vol. 22, No. 86, pp. 99–109.

Boyns, T. and Edwards, J.R. (1997), 'The Construction of Cost Accounting Systems in Britain to 1900: The Case of the Coal, Iron and Steel Industries', *Business History*, Vol. 39, No. 3, pp. 1–29.

Brief, R.P. (1965), 'Nineteenth century accounting error', *Journal of Accounting Research*, Vol. 3, pp. 12–31.

Chatfield, Michael (1977), *A History of Accounting Thought*, (Robert E. Krieger Publishing, New York).

Church, R.A., Baldwin, T.J. and Berry, R.H. (1994), 'Accounting for profitability at the Consett Iron Company before 1914: measurement, sources, and uses', *Economic History Review*, XLVII, 4 (1994), pp. 703–24.

Cottrell, P.L. (1980), *Industrial Finance 1830–1914; The Finance and Organisation of English Manufacturing Industry*, (Methuen, London).

Edey, H.C. (1956), 'Company Accounting in the Nineteenth and Twentieth Centuries', *Certified Accountants Journal*, 48. Reprinted (1979) in T.A. Lee and R.H. Parker, *The Evolution of Corporate Financial Reporting*, pp. 222–30 (Nelson, London).

Edey, H.C. and Panitpakdi, P. (1956), 'British Company Accounting and the Law 1844–1900' in A.C. Littleton and B.S. Yamey (eds.), *Studies in the History of Accounting* (Sweet & Maxwell, London).

Edwards, J.R. (1989), *A History of Financial Accounting* (Routledge, London).

Edwards, J.R. and Barber, C. (1979), 'Dowlais Iron Company: Accounting Policies and Procedures for Profit Measurement and Reporting Purposes', *Accounting & Business Research*, Spring 1979, pp. 139–51.

Edwards, J.R. and Webb, K. (1982), 'The Influence of Company Law on Corporate Reporting Procedures, 1865–1929: An Exemplification', *Business History,* November 1982, pp. 259–79.

Edwards, J.R. and Webb, K.M. (1985), 'Use of Table A by Companies Registering Under the Companies Act 1862', *Accounting & Business Research,* Summer 1985, pp. 177–95.

Jones, S. and Aiken, M. (1994), 'The Significance of the Profit and Loss Account in Nineteenth Century Britain: A Reassessment', *Abacus*, September 1994, pp. 196–223.

Lee, G.A. (1973), *Modern Financial Accounting* (Nelson, UK).

Lee, G.A. (1975), 'The Concept of Profit in British Accounting, 1760–1900', *Business History Review,* Vol. 49, pp. 6–36.

Lee, T.A. (1978), 'Company Financial Statements: An Essay in Business History 1830–1950' in S. Marriner (ed.), *Business and Businessmen: Studies in Business, Economic and Accounting History* (Liverpool University Press).

Lee, T.A. (1984), *Cash Flow Accounting* (Van Nostrand Reinhold, UK).

Macve, Richard H., (1986), 'Some Glosses on Greek and Roman Accounting', *History of Political Thought,* 1986, p. 233.

Marriner, S. (1980), 'Company financial statements as source material for business historians', *Business History,* Vol. 22, pp. 202–35.

Matheson, Ewing (1884), *The Depreciation of Factories, Mines and Industrial Undertakings and their Valuation* (London).

Napier, C.J. (1989), 'Research Directions in Accounting History', *British Accounting Review,* Vol. 21, No. 3, pp. 237–54.

Parker, R.H. (1990), 'Regulating British Corporate Financial Reporting in the Late Nineteenth Century', *Accounting, Business and Financial History,* Vol. 1, No. 1, pp. 51–71.

Parker, R.H. (1991), 'Misleading Accounts? Pitfalls for Historians', *Business History,* Vol. 33, No. 4, October 1991, pp. 1–18.

Pitts, M.V. (1998), 'Did dividends dictate depreciation in British coal companies 1864–1914?', *Accounting History*, Vol. 3, No. 2, November 1998, pp. 37–67.

Pollard, Sidney (1963), 'Capital Accounting in the Industrial Revolution', *Yorkshire Bulletin of Economic and Social Research*, November 1963.

Pollins, H. (1956), 'Aspects of Railway Accounting Before 1868' in A.C. Littleton, and B.S. Yamey (eds.), *Studies in the History of Accounting* (Sweet & Maxwell, London).

Wale, J. (1990), 'How reliable were reported profits and asset values in the period 1890–1914? Case studies from the British coal industry', *Accounting and Business Research*, Vol. 20, pp. 253–68.

Yamey, B.S. (1960), 'The Development of Company Accounting Conventions', *Three Banks Review*, September 1960, pp. 3–18.

Yamey, B.S. (1962a), 'Some Topics in the History of Financial Accounting in England 1500–1900' in W.T. Baxter and S. Davidson (eds.), *Studies in Accounting Theory* (Sweet & Maxwell, London).

Yamey, B.S. (1962b), 'The Case Law Relating to Company Dividends' in W.T. Baxter and S. Davidson (eds.), *Studies in Accounting Theory* (Sweet & Maxwell, London).

PART 2

COMPANY CASH FLOW STATEMENTS

INDEX OF COMPANIES

BELL BROTHERS LTD
FUNDING 1873-1914

	Incorporated 1872 and 1898										
Financing for year to 31 September	1873	1874	1875	1876	1877	1878	1879	1880	1881	1882	1883
Financing for year to 31 December											
Internal Finance											
Operating Profit before interest and depreciation	321341	176985	76155	37758	37276	49273	34350	128851	100370	111838	86314
invested in											
Stock	86468	15554	-24230	8525	-27604	1296	-2996	29315	1072	2394	29316
Debtors	171517	-88502	-9427	-25128	-5729	-2826	14246	23383	7316	11492	8472
Creditors	-141331	10154	-8858	8783	51056	18010	-726	-3174	-6189	16151	-8084
Change in Working Capital	116654	-62794	-42515	-7820	17723	16480	10524	49524	2199	30037	29704
Cash Flow from operations	204687	239779	118670	45578	19553	32793	23826	79327	98171	81801	56610
invested in											
Cash & Bank	41792	-41621	-16716	-18769	6241	23170	-12599	14348	-12241	9189	-6531
Fixed Assets	972467	225498	74699	30482	677	5583	2189	11670	19111	22173	16530
Free Cash	-809572	55902	60687	33865	12635	4040	34236	53309	91301	50439	46611
External Finance											
Shareholders											
Issue of Ordinary Share Capital	780000	187760	0	0	0	0	0	0	0	0	0
Dividends Paid	0	-390000	-42339	-24194	0	0	0	-30242	-51416	-42339	-27218
	780000	**-202240**	**-42339**	**-24194**	**0**	**0**	**0**	**-30242**	**-51416**	**-42339**	**-27218**
Lenders											
Issue/Repayment of Loans	29572	154887	-5025	3524	-66	8791	-22171	-14861	-32662	-1294	-12569
Interest	0	-8549	-13323	-13195	-12569	-12831	-12065	-8206	-7223	-6806	-6824
	29572	**146338**	**-18348**	**-9671**	**-12635**	**-4040**	**-34236**	**-23067**	**-39885**	**-8100**	**-19393**
Externally generated funds	809572	-55902	-60687	-33865	-12635	-4040	-34236	-53309	-91301	-50439	-46611

BELL BROTHERS LTD
FUNDING 1873-1914

	1884	1885	1886	1887	1888	1889	1890	1891	1892	1893	1894
Financing for year to 31 September											
Financing for year to 31 December											
Internal Finance											
Operating Profit before interest and depreciation	**77195**	**64206**	**39037**	**38971**	**42682**	**171766**	**102951**	**74856**	**38223**	**47248**	**58827**
invested in											
Stock	43339	-61535	29300	8969	-56627	5146	92450	-28565	-28749	-26364	-12000
Debtors	-54645	35798	-6936	15788	50820	-72149	-1006	-6342	153457	85784	46960
Creditors	17940	-3534	-2209	7502	-8193	-14250	-27251	16459	6021	18419	-3052
Change in Working Capital	**6634**	**-29271**	**20155**	**32259**	**-14000**	**-81253**	**64193**	**-18448**	**130729**	**77839**	**31908**
Cash Flow from operations	**70561**	**93477**	**18882**	**6712**	**56682**	**253019**	**38758**	**93304**	**-92506**	**-30591**	**26919**
invested in											
Cash & Bank	-21230	35414	-24886	-7602	25659	120163	-186779	18215	-101718	-27006	19856
Fixed Assets	42968	30719	20491	15848	28243	62498	116197	55137	-16455	-8948	4677
Free Cash	**48823**	**27344**	**23277**	**-1534**	**2780**	**70358**	**109340**	**19952**	**25667**	**5363**	**2386**
External Finance											
Shareholders											
Issue of Ordinary Share Capital	0	0	0	0	0	0	0	0	0	0	0
Dividends Paid	-27218	-6048	-18145	0	0	-57462	-72582	-12097	-25705	-6048	-6048
	-27218	**-6048**	**-18145**	**0**	**0**	**-57462**	**-72582**	**-12097**	**-25705**	**-6048**	**-6048**
Lenders											
Issue/Repayment of Loans	-16190	-15173	-1304	5718	1617	-9957	-35243	-3823	2678	8070	12013
Interest	-5415	-6123	-3828	-4184	-4397	-2939	-1515	-4032	-2640	-7385	-8351
	-21605	**-21296**	**-5132**	**1534**	**-2780**	**-12896**	**-36758**	**-7855**	**38**	**685**	**3662**
Externally generated funds	**-48823**	**-27344**	**-23277**	**1534**	**-2780**	**-70358**	**-109340**	**-19952**	**-25667**	**-5363**	**-2386**

BELL BROTHERS LTD
FUNDING 1873-1914

	1895	1896	1897	1898 15 months	Incorporated 1872 and 1898 1899	1900	1901	1902	1903	1904	1905
Financing for year to 31 September											
Financing for year to 31 December											
Internal Finance											
Operating Profit before interest and depreciation	68190	80502	99796	118651	139916	355993	69991	123930	97975	62208	97799
invested in											
Stock	5101	-9622	-7430	10701	122592	29332	-26555	-7656	-4495	-6024	24765
Debtors	-14951	13772	-1608	-4414	9068	8879	-16204	-21689	3466	1248	-1881
Creditors	-358	-3036	-14265	2438	-29396	-37265	9424	11124	-19032	-2773	-6061
Change in Working Capital	-10208	1114	-23303	8725	102264	946	-33335	-18221	-20061	-7549	16823
Cash Flow from operations	78398	79388	123099	109926	37652	355047	103326	142151	118036	69757	80976
invested in											
Cash & Bank	-14092	42069	51061	45601	124903	-54862	-54233	22163	-6076	11647	-28114
Fixed Assets	181	8911	36864	28987	221878	284909	88059	87988	45612	51610	39590
Free Cash	92309	28408	35174	35338	-309129	125000	69500	32000	78500	6500	69500
External Finance											
Shareholders											
Issue of Ordinary Share Capital	-87760	0	0	0	-40000	60000	60000	30000	0	60000	0
Dividends Paid	-12808	-22500	-30000	-36000	-40175	-165000	-109500	-42000	-58500	-46500	-49500
	-100568	-22500	-30000	-36000	-80175	-105000	-49500	-12000	-58500	13500	-49500
Lenders											
Issue/Repayment of Loans	18118	3605	1628	5654	414463	0	0	0	0	0	0
Interest	-9859	-9513	-6802	-4992	-25159	-20000	-20000	-20000	-20000	-20000	-20000
	8259	-5908	-5174	662	389304	-20000	-20000	-20000	-20000	-20000	-20000
Externally generated funds	-92309	-28408	-35174	-35338	309129	-125000	-69500	-32000	-78500	-6500	-69500

BELL BROTHERS LTD
FUNDING 1873-1914

	1906	1907	1908	1909	1910	1911	1912	1913	1914
Financing for year to 31 September									
Financing for year to 31 December									
Internal Finance									
Operating Profit before	**142107**	**152245**	**77549**	**102375**	**116701**	**82406**	**91756**	**139562**	**54088**
interest and depreciation									
invested in									
Stock	-25744	18844	-13506	-3339	11762	-14197	-14811	25875	-30424
Debtors	6130	-5839	-14430	2818	1175	-3306	9265	10085	-20592
Creditors	16849	-29156	9694	1748	-7206	8412	4948	-18565	-8234
Change in Working Capital	**-2765**	**-16151**	**-18242**	**1227**	**5731**	**-9091**	**-598**	**17395**	**-59250**
Cash Flow from operations	**144872**	**168396**	**95791**	**101148**	**110970**	**91497**	**92354**	**122167**	**113338**
invested in									
Cash & Bank	38263	-3143	-5997	8501	1792	-33145	14699	-1083	-29215
Fixed Assets	-24751	96819	21818	26657	26560	43371	18169	107845	65042
Free Cash	**131360**	**74720**	**79970**	**65990**	**82618**	**81271**	**59486**	**15405**	**77511**
External Finance									
Shareholders									
Issue of Ordinary Share Capital	0	0	0	0	0	0	0	30000	0
Dividends Paid	-55500	-57000	-50250	-48750	-57000	-51000	-37500	-57000	-43960
	-55500	**-57000**	**-50250**	**-48750**	**-57000**	**-51000**	**-37500**	**-27000**	**-43960**
Lenders									
Issue/Repayment of Loans	-57000	0	-12000	0	-8500	-13480	-5625	27276	-18417
Interest	-18860	-17720	-17720	-17240	-17118	-16791	-16361	-15681	-15134
	-75860	**-17720**	**-29720**	**-17240**	**-25618**	**-30271**	**-21986**	**11595**	**-33551**
Externally generated funds	**-131360**	**-74720**	**-79970**	**-65990**	**-82618**	**-81271**	**-59486**	**-15405**	**-77511**

BELL BROTHERS LTD
FUNDING 1873-1914

Financing for year to 31 September Financing for year to 31 December Internal Finance	Summary 1873-1889	percentage 1873-1889	Summary 1890-1914	percentage 1890-1914	Summary 1873-1914	percentage 1874-1914
Operating Profit before interest and depreciation	1594368	815.54	2595845	237.25	4190213	466.28
invested in						
Stock	87702	44.86	81941	7.49	169643	18.88
Debtors	73490	37.59	239845	21.92	313335	34.87
Creditors	-66952	-34.25	-100114	-9.15	-167066	-18.59
Change in Working Capital	94240	48.20	221672	20.26	315912	35.15
Cash Flow from operations	1500128	767.33	2374173	216.99	3874301	431.13
invested in						
Cash & Bank	113781	58.20	-146693	-13.41	-32912	-3.66
Fixed Assets	1581846	809.13	1426727	130.40	3008573	334.79
Free Cash	-195499	-100.00	1094139	100.00	898640	100.00
External Finance						
Shareholders						
Issue of Ordinary Share Capital	967760	495.02	112240	10.26	1080000	120.18
Dividends Paid	-716621	-366.56	-1192923	-109.03	-1909544	-212.49
	251139	128.46	-1080683	-98.77	-829544	-92.31
Lenders						
Issue/Repayment of Loans	72837	37.26	339417	31.02	412254	45.88
Interest	-128477	-65.72	-352873	-32.25	-481350	-53.56
	-55640	-28.46	-13456	-1.23	-69096	-7.69
Externally generated funds	195499	100.00	-1094139	-100.00	-898640	-100.00

BOLCKOW VAUGHAN AND COMPANY LTD
FUNDING 1865-1914

	Incorporated 1864 1865	1866	1867	1868	1869	1870	1871	1872	1873	1874
Financing for year to 31 December										
Financing for year to 30 June										
Internal Finance										
Operating Profit before										
interest and depreciation	**93171**	**55656**	**71674**	**144426**	**138658**	**136137**	**171742**	**294020**	**503837**	**222441**
invested in										
Stock	162494	58105	53976	-57933	23162	27668	11837	154505	145228	-253626
Debtors	155114	-15698	-565	-3713	-23093	-8498	68542	46923	1552	-45902
Creditors	-156479	1769	-111722	-1559	150447	-54747	-42524	-57390	-94506	166704
Change in Working Capital	161129	44176	-58311	-63205	150516	-35577	37855	144038	52274	-132824
Cash Flow from operations	**-67958**	**11480**	**129985**	**207631**	**-11858**	**171714**	**133887**	**149982**	**451563**	**355265**
invested in										
Cash & Bank	42076	-38863	1797	58544	-14241	-25786	-7873	-13227	1926	34212
Fixed Assets	914344	56101	114018	-10877	-46979	-26461	118417	424397	81126	232276
Free cash	**-1024378**	**-5758**	**14170**	**159964**	**49362**	**223961**	**23343**	**-261188**	**368511**	**88777**
External Finance										
Shareholders										
Issue of Ordinary Share Capital	699510	75940	131825	6250	-1068	-312	0	124540	50	-350
Dividends Paid	0	-69985	-48621	-72297	-75078	-137538	-129000	-195500	-302587	-326230
	699510	**5955**	**83204**	**-66047**	**-76146**	**-137850**	**-129000**	**-70960**	**-302537**	**-326580**
Lenders										
Issue/Repayment of Loans	324868	-197	-97374	-93917	26784	-86111	107783	337494	-58361	252228
Interest	0	0	0	0	0	0	-2126	-5346	-7613	-14425
(deb. interest estimated 4.5% pre 1881)										
	324868	**-197**	**-97374**	**-93917**	**26784**	**-86111**	**105657**	**332148**	**-65974**	**237803**
Externally generated funds	**1024378**	**5758**	**-14170**	**-159964**	**-49362**	**-223961**	**-23343**	**261188**	**-368511**	**-88777**

BOLCKOW VAUGHAN AND COMPANY LTD
FUNDING 1865-1914

Financing for year to 31 December / Financing for year to 30 June	1875	1876	1877	1878	1879	1880	1881	1882	1883	1884
Internal Finance										
Operating Profit before interest and depreciation invested in	168751	161619	152516	150601	92797	409442	305329	311929	204751	160281
Stock	-6356	49831	204517	-13017	-42360	51382	53004	25436	-92909	54503
Debtors	-6201	71488	-38092	11746	-8053	-1948	81736	30090	-76182	-91113
Creditors	-45898	-9470	-42796	91622	-142476	-78684	-105206	48698	92891	-86664
Change in Working Capital	-58455	111849	123629	90351	-192889	-29250	29534	104224	-76200	-123274
Cash Flow from operations invested in	227206	49770	28887	60250	285686	438692	275795	207705	280951	283555
Cash & Bank	-35429	885	883	-457	2104	-2688	-1988	1322	-891	-1140
Fixed Assets	100049	179677	166021	49707	150820	281835	143697	193675	84851	82320
Free cash	162586	-130792	-138017	11000	132762	159545	134086	12708	196991	202375
External Finance										
Shareholders										
Issue of Ordinary Share Capital	0	328450	302805	154110	188405	145355	130	231770	61723	5607
Dividends Paid	-170501	-131438	-147873	-139757	-70090	-237553	-247675	-249243	-193943	-102920
	-170501	197012	154932	14353	118315	-92198	-247545	-17473	-132220	-97313
Lenders										
Issue/Repayment of Loans	29178	-44004	5201	-2980	-230030	-46478	134915	27700	-42300	-83820
Interest	-21263	-22216	-22116	-22373	-21047	-20869	-21456	-22935	-22471	-21242
(deb. interest estimated 4.5% pre 1881)	7916	-66220	-16915	-25353	-251077	-67347	113459	4765	-64771	-105062
Externally generated funds	-162586	130792	138017	-11000	-132762	-159545	-134086	-12708	-196991	-202375

BOLCKOW VAUGHAN AND COMPANY LTD
FUNDING 1865-1914

	1885	1886	1887	1888	1889	1890	1891	1892	1893	1894
Financing for year to 31 December										
Financing for year to 30 June										
Internal Finance										
Operating Profit before interest and depreciation	**140564**	**147970**	**179743**	**161385**	**316996**	**329710**	**86243**	**81110**	**153250**	**147660**
invested in										
Stock	-33036	73791	-9729	-36111	24531	58182	-86416	-28011	-40275	16592
Debtors	-18007	119674	-46668	989	-22528	7380	-40000	2830	-9972	-15060
Creditors	80837	-86544	158762	-38543	20452	-8854	27398	-15593	141114	-2536
Change in Working Capital	29794	106921	102365	-73665	22455	56708	-99018	-40774	90867	-1004
Cash Flow from operations	**110770**	**41049**	**77378**	**235050**	**294541**	**273002**	**185261**	**121884**	**62383**	**148664**
invested in										
Cash & Bank	3900	3561	-7107	-234	1539	-1454	-101	74	46990	-19497
Fixed Assets	50729	60879	5141	40728	35983	-9642	-29375	-29480	-50054	-50536
Free cash	**56141**	**-23391**	**79344**	**194556**	**257019**	**284098**	**214737**	**151290**	**65447**	**218697**
External Finance										
Shareholders										
Issue of Ordinary Share Capital	40	140	13460	0	0	0	0	0	0	0
Dividends Paid	-103044	-103048	-103661	-117795	-186453	-213916	-117795	-104063	-104064	-104064
	-103004	**-102908**	**-90201**	**-117795**	**-186453**	**-213916**	**-117795**	**-104063**	**-104064**	**-104064**
Lenders										
Issue/Repayment of Loans	65526	146543	33950	-52843	-46750	-49005	-78190	-32430	54080	-99030
Interest	-18663	-20244	-23093	-23918	-23816	-21177	-18752	-14797	-15463	-15603
(deb. interest estimated 4.5% pre 1881)	**46863**	**126299**	**10857**	**-76761**	**-70566**	**-70182**	**-96942**	**-47227**	**38617**	**-114633**
Externally generated funds	**-56141**	**23391**	**-79344**	**-194556**	**-257019**	**-284098**	**-214737**	**-151290**	**-65447**	**-218697**

BOLCKOW VAUGHAN AND COMPANY LTD
FUNDING 1865-1914

	1895	1896	1897	1898	1899	18 months 1901	1902	1903	1904	1905
Financing for year to 31 December										
Financing for year to 30 June										
Internal Finance										
Operating Profit before interest and depreciation invested in	171818	298049	284477	237434	485588	630100	195265	290551	211443	225672
Stock	33432	-37624	-4585	41123	-5919	-2995	-32134	22585	14669	-5375
Debtors	-8109	33995	41510	-36140	77371	-21047	-22651	-8316	-17222	19737
Creditors	-16749	-15013	-5592	29202	-84977	11943	-14400	-3079	-35122	-37099
Change in Working Capital	8574	-18642	31333	34185	-13525	-12099	-69185	11190	-37675	-22737
Cash Flow from operations invested in	163244	316691	253144	203249	499113	642199	264450	279361	249118	248409
Cash & Bank	69083	68434	11947	-51713	10581	116455	-40233	-162274	-332323	-315108
Fixed Assets	-51517	-24408	-21479	393	219530	29059	86734	268913	408719	512275
Free cash	**145678**	**272665**	**262676**	**254569**	**269002**	**496685**	**217949**	**172722**	**172722**	**51242**
External Finance										
Shareholders										
Issue of Ordinary Share Capital	0	0	0	0	0	0	0	0	0	0
Dividends Paid	-104064	-172720	-186452	-172721	-186452	-431690	-213915	-172722	-172722	-172720
	-104064	**-172720**	**-186452**	**-172721**	**-186452**	**-431690**	**-213915**	**-172722**	**-172722**	**-172720**
Lenders										
Issue/Repayment of Loans	-26714	-86986	-64980	-74400	-82550	-62800	-4000	0	0	122200
Interest	-14900	-12959	-11244	-7448	0	-2195	-34	0	0	-722
(deb. interest estimated 4.5% pre 1881)										
	-41614	**-99945**	**-76224**	**-81848**	**-82550**	**-64995**	**-4034**	**0**	**0**	**121478**
Externally generated funds	**-145678**	**-272665**	**-262676**	**-254569**	**-269002**	**-496685**	**-217949**	**-172722**	**-172722**	**-51242**

BOLCKOW VAUGHAN AND COMPANY LTD
FUNDING 1865-1914

Financing for year to 31 December
Financing for year to 30 June

	1906	1907	1908	1909	1910	1911	1912	1913	1914
Internal Finance									
Operating Profit before interest and depreciation	356938	694812	456004	333837	402287	474571	302364	699144	419999
invested in									
Stock	14044	26147	589	39875	35305	35223	-139069	222645	-58098
Debtors	52490	12565	-33135	-66140	80218	-60554	111055	-79544	39799
Creditors	-44390	-68569	-4138	14262	-19169	64642	30275	-87947	131140
Change in Working Capital	22144	-29857	-36684	-12003	96354	39311	2261	55154	112841
Cash Flow from operations	334794	724669	492688	345840	305933	435260	300103	643990	307158
invested in									
Cash & Bank	337607	352319	-32857	-22754	-16571	63751	-106105	134941	-259984
Fixed Assets	164840	262225	235593	288903	162410	164311	163909	208164	145458
Free cash	-167653	110125	289952	79691	160094	207198	242299	300885	421684
External Finance									
Shareholders									
Issue of Ordinary Share Capital	0	0	0	0	0	0	0	0	0
Dividends Paid	-172722	-200185	-310036	-200184	-172721	-200184	-200184	-172721	-310037
	-172722	**-200185**	**-310036**	**-200184**	**-172721**	**-200184**	**-200184**	**-172721**	**-310037**
Lenders									
Issue/Repayment of Loans	353700	112000	44700	148200	45500	26000	-8600	-97400	-83700
Interest	-13325	-21940	-24616	-27707	-32873	-33014	-33515	-30764	-27947
(deb. interest estimated 4.5% pre 1881)									
	340375	**90060**	**20084**	**120493**	**12627**	**-7014**	**-42115**	**-128164**	**-111647**
Externally generated funds	167653	-110125	-289952	-79691	-160094	-207198	-242299	-300885	-421684

BOLCKOW VAUGHAN AND COMPANY LTD
FUNDING 1865-1914

Financing for year to 31 December / Financing for year to 30 June	Summary 1865-1889	percentage 1865-1889	Summary 1890-1914	percentage 1890-1914	Summary 1865-1914	percentage 1865-1914
Internal Finance						
Operating Profit before interest and depreciation	4896435	518.87	7968326	162.80	12864761	220.36
invested in						
Stock	628893	66.64	119910	2.45	748803	12.83
Debtors	181593	19.24	61060	1.25	242653	4.16
Creditors	-343026	-36.35	-13251	-0.27	-356277	-6.10
Change in Working Capital	467460	49.54	167719	3.43	635179	10.88
Cash Flow from operations	4428975	469.33	7800607	159.38	12229582	209.48
invested in						
Cash & Bank	2825	0.30	-148792	-3.04	-145967	-2.50
Fixed Assets	3482474	369.03	3054945	62.42	6537419	111.98
Free cash	943676	100.00	4894454	100.00	5838130	100.00
External Finance						
Shareholders						
Issue of Ordinary Share Capital	2468380	261.57	0	0.00	2468380	42.28
Dividends Paid	-3661830	-388.04	-4569054	-93.35	-8230884	-140.98
	-1193450	-126.47	-4569054	-93.35	-5762504	-98.70
Lenders						
Issue/Repayment of Loans	607005	64.32	55595	1.14	662600	11.35
Interest	-357231	-37.86	-380995	-7.78	-738226	-12.64
(deb. interest estimated 4.5% pre 1881)	249774	26.47	-325400	-6.65	-75626	-1.30
Externally generated funds	-943676	-100.00	-4894454	-100.00	-5838130	-100.00

BUTTERLEY COMPANY LTD
FUNDING 1881-1914

Incorporated 1888

Financing for year to 25 March	1881	1882	1883	1884	1885	1886	1887	1888	1889	1890	1891	1892
	cumulative figures to 1881											
Internal Finance	*balancing figure*											
Operating Profit before interest and depreciation invested in	*15317*	14221	31615	21404	4971	-11010	-10018	-33012		94930	73787	53640
Stock	273519	-26915	66696	-32435	16393	-29285	-12532	-62572		5323	35248	-6082
Debtors	120211	12393	11818	146	-5065	23494	12921	2819		20251	-5338	10884
Creditors	-54420	-2395	-26252	20111	9314	1313	1884	-8340		30006	-4479	-5599
Change in Working Capital	**339310**	**-16917**	**52262**	**-12178**	**20642**	**-4478**	**2273**	**-68093**		**55580**	**25431**	**-797**
Cash Flow from operations invested in	**-323993**	**31138**	**-20647**	**33582**	**-15671**	**-6532**	**-12291**	**35081**		**39350**	**48356**	**54437**
Bank & Cash	-33522	-23222	10061	1800	15159	-11253	-31069	2914		-212	-374	541
Fixed Assets	1098099	33527	-56796	8704	-70954	-44202	-13931	6339		11915	12410	22603
Free Cash	**-1388570**	**20833**	**26088**	**23078**	**40124**	**48923**	**32709**	**25828**		**27647**	**36320**	**31293**
External Finance									capital conversion			
Shareholders									shares to loan			
Partnership Capital	1428275	0	-5693	-180	-282	-2679	0	0	*balancing figure*	-122844	0	0
Profits Distributed	-42000	-20833	-68500	-19500	-25250	-15050	-39479	-58952		-5467	-21868	-16401
	1386275	**-20833**	**-74193**	**-19680**	**-25532**	**-17729**	**-39479**	**-58952**		**-128311**	**-21868**	**-16401**
Lenders												
Issue/Repayment of Loans	2295	0	50569	0	-10804	-28760	8365	36791		123544	0	0
Interest		0	-2464	-3398	-3788	-2434	-1595	-3667		-22880	-14452	-14892
	2295	**0**	**48105**	**-3398**	**-14592**	**-31194**	**6770**	**33124**		**100664**	**-14452**	**-14892**
Externally generated funds	**1388570**	**-20833**	**-26088**	**-23078**	**-40124**	**-48923**	**-32709**	**-25828**		**-27647**	**-36320**	**-31293**

BUTTERLEY COMPANY LTD
FUNDING 1881-1914

Financing for year to 25 March	1893	1894	1895	1896	1897	1898	1899	1900	1901	1902	1903	1904
Internal Finance												
Operating Profit before interest and depreciation	**37272**	**25427**	**27060**	**10595**	**46853**	**53609**	**92716**	**200529**	**288046**	**75681**	**87977**	**52916**
invested in												
Stock	22745	-15173	13512	-4804	-8185	-27744	26957	2536	51336	-49552	-5232	-74
Debtors	-7922	10475	1716	11097	14025	17284	-3577	66048	-6269	-39121	-29185	19781
Creditors	-962	-14596	-15905	-30456	7556	40119	25745	47944	1723	11790	11022	-10867
Change in Working Capital	**13861**	**-19294**	**-677**	**-24163**	**13396**	**29659**	**49125**	**116528**	**46790**	**-76883**	**-23395**	**8840**
Cash Flow from operations	**23411**	**44721**	**27737**	**34758**	**33457**	**23950**	**43591**	**84001**	**241256**	**152564**	**111372**	**44076**
invested in												
Bank & Cash	283	-904	457	724	2173	3941	-6992	21134	9978	13549	-2802	-25400
Fixed Assets	-7248	20325	12182	20770	10247	-5443	16061	18689	113682	35442	57071	11688
Free Cash	**30376**	**25300**	**15098**	**13264**	**21037**	**25452**	**34522**	**44178**	**117596**	**103573**	**57103**	**57788**
External Finance												
Shareholders												
Issue of ordinary Share Capital	0	0	0	0	0	0	0	0	0	0	0	0
Dividends Paid	-16401	-10934	0	-6834	-5467	-10934	-21868	-32802	-109340	-95673	-49203	-49203
	-16401	**-10934**	**0**	**-6834**	**-5467**	**-10934**	**-21868**	**-32802**	**-109340**	**-95673**	**-49203**	**-49203**
Lenders												
Issue/Repayment of Loans	0	0	0	9000	0	0	0	0	0	0	0	0
Interest	-13975	-14366	-15098	-15430	-15570	-14518	-12654	-11376	-8256	-7900	-7900	-8585
	-13975	**-14366**	**-15098**	**-6430**	**-15570**	**-14518**	**-12654**	**-11376**	**-8256**	**-7900**	**-7900**	**-8585**
Externally generated funds	**-30376**	**-25300**	**-15098**	**-13264**	**-21037**	**-25452**	**-34522**	**-44178**	**-117596**	**-103573**	**-57103**	**-57788**

BUTTERLEY COMPANY LTD
FUNDING 1881-1914

Financing for year to 25 March	1905	1906	1907	1908	1909	1910	1911	1912	1913	1914
Internal Finance										
Operating Profit before interest and depreciation	**46912**	**96217**	**49507**	**169582**	**86763**	**44012**	**78912**	**131636**	**197541**	**180301**
invested in										
Stock	15208	-22588	733	16191	3344	-14743	22745	-5124	-13207	11291
Debtors	-22585	41389	-3353	10460	-17803	-566	5078	-43350	72892	-8181
Creditors	-1476	-6008	-1930	10447	-587	10248	4782	13507	-38124	-1131
Change in Working Capital	**-8853**	**12793**	**-4550**	**37098**	**-15046**	**-5061**	**32605**	**-34967**	**21561**	**1979**
Cash Flow from operations	**55765**	**83424**	**54057**	**132484**	**101809**	**49073**	**46307**	**166603**	**175980**	**178322**
invested in										
Bank & Cash	-7222	-32219	-26248	15202	-6810	-31305	-15448	83015	78322	-9326
Fixed Assets	26749	81672	36780	40105	51868	41464	22415	41949	32015	79158
Free Cash	**36238**	**33971**	**43525**	**77177**	**56751**	**38914**	**39340**	**41639**	**65643**	**108490**
External Finance										
Shareholders										
Issue of ordinary Share Capital	0	0	0	0	0	0	0	0	0	0
Dividends Paid	-27335	-24601	-32802	-66469	-46470	-27335	-27335	-30069	-57404	-101140
	-27335	**-24601**	**-32802**	**-66469**	**-46470**	**-27335**	**-27335**	**-30069**	**-57404**	**-101140**
Lenders										
Issue/Repayment of Loans	0	0	0	0	0	0	0	0	0	0
Interest	-8903	-9370	-10723	-10708	-10281	-11579	-12005	-11570	-8239	-7350
	-8903	**-9370**	**-10723**	**-10708**	**-10281**	**-11579**	**-12005**	**-11570**	**-8239**	**-7350**
Externally generated funds	**-36238**	**-33971**	**-43525**	**-77177**	**-56751**	**-38914**	**-39340**	**-41639**	**-65643**	**-108490**

BUTTERLEY COMPANY LTD
FUNDING 1881-1914

Financing for year to 25 March	Partnership Summary 1881-1889	percentage 1881-1889	Company Summary 1890-1914	percentage 1890-1914	Summary 1881-1914	percentage 1881-1914
Internal Finance						
Operating Profit before interest and depreciation invested in	33488	2.86	2302421	194.75	2335909	20767.33
Stock	192869	16.47	54661	4.62	247530	2200.66
Debtors	178737	15.26	114130	9.65	292867	2603.73
Creditors	-58785	-5.02	82769	7.00	23984	213.23
Change in Working Capital	312821	26.71	251560	21.28	564381	5017.61
Cash Flow from operations invested in	-279333	-23.85	2050861	173.47	1771528	15749.72
Bank & Cash	-69132	-5.90	64057	5.42	-5075	-45.12
Fixed Assets	960786	82.05	804569	68.05	1765355	15694.83
Free Cash	-1170987	-100.00	1182235	100.00	11248	100.00
External Finance						
Shareholders						
Issue of ordinary Share Capital	1419441	121.22	-122844	-10.39	1296597	11527.36
Dividends Paid	-289564	-24.73	-893355	-75.56	-1182919	-10516.71
	1129877	96.49	-1016199	-85.96	113678	1010.65
Lenders						
Issue/Repayment of Loans	58456	4.99	132544	11.21	191000	1698.08
Interest	-17346	-1.48	-298580	-25.26	-315926	-2808.73
	41110	3.51	-166036	-14.04	-124926	-1110.65
Externally generated funds	1170987	100.00	-1182235	-100.00	-11248	-100.00

CANNOCK CHASE COLLIERY COMPANY LTD
FUNDING 1860-1911

Financing for year to 31 December	Incorporated 1859 1860	1861	1862	1863	1864	1865	1866	1867	1868	1869	1870
Internal Finance											
Operating Profit before interest and depreciation	**11002**	**9453**	**12796**	**23231**	**57255**	**34195**	**37340**	**51131**	**35764**	**39197**	**41093**
invested in											
Stock	339	564	-175	305	-51	111	4	2270	1516	-1520	376
Debtors	26217	-9793	8864	16895	3742	2266	4067	9762	73	1276	23042
Creditors	-6299	-1682	-1556	-184	-1620	1763	-2108	-4947	1776	-334	-2307
Change in Working Capital	**20257**	**-10911**	**7133**	**17016**	**2071**	**4140**	**1963**	**7085**	**3365**	**-578**	**21111**
Cash Flow from operations	**-9255**	**20364**	**5663**	**6215**	**55184**	**30055**	**35377**	**44046**	**32399**	**39775**	**19982**
invested in											
Bank & Cash	-933	-6272	-8411	-10326	-1327	-4537	7519	-5824	-499	1146	-5374
Fixed Assets	87333	19481	15661	8895	20375	6236	10126	26062	-17937	9991	7452
Free Cash	**-95655**	**7155**	**-1587**	**7646**	**36136**	**28356**	**17732**	**23808**	**50835**	**28638**	**17904**
External Finance											
Shareholders											
Issue of Ordinary Share Capital	100000	-800	9044	11156	-1600	-1600	18400	16300	-3700	-3700	26300
Dividends Paid	-4345	-6355	-7457	-18802	-34536	-26756	-36132	-40108	-47135	-24938	-44204
	95655	**-7155**	**1587**	**-7646**	**-36136**	**-28356**	**-17732**	**-23808**	**-50835**	**-28638**	**-17904**
Lenders											
Issue/Repayment of Loans	0	0	0	0	0	0	0	0	0	0	0
Interest	0	0	0	0	0	0	0	0	0	0	0
	0	**0**	**0**	**0**	**0**	**0**	**0**	**0**	**0**	**0**	**0**
Externally generated funds	**95655**	**-7155**	**1587**	**-7646**	**-36136**	**-28356**	**-17732**	**-23808**	**-50835**	**-28638**	**-17904**

CANNOCK CHASE COLLIERY COMPANY LTD
FUNDING 1860-1911

Financing for year to 31 December	1871	1872	1873	1874	1875	1876	1877	1878	1879	1880	1881
Internal Finance											
Operating Profit before interest and depreciation	**44622**	**92798**	**211466**	**55201**	**42135**	**28018**	**11200**	**-9203**	**6032**	**10484**	**4947**
invested in											
Stock	1619	3965	5765	-1653	6748	3034	-2668	-1867	-806	3232	1376
Debtors	-3854	6333	44155	-39044	-21504	-13077	-718	-14751	5485	163	1262
Creditors	1219	-15787	10159	6289	-1437	5945	-2958	1518	-4162	-3056	-3535
Change in Working Capital	**-1016**	**-5489**	**60079**	**-34408**	**-16193**	**-4098**	**-6344**	**-15100**	**517**	**339**	**-897**
Cash Flow from operations	**45638**	**98287**	**151387**	**89609**	**58328**	**32116**	**17544**	**5897**	**5515**	**10145**	**5844**
invested in											
Bank & Cash	13014	28267	25544	-32745	-4436	6997	4923	-7538	-2688	1057	-8346
Fixed Assets	9264	12911	14326	15718	19387	9170	1522	-976	-382	-1747	430
Free Cash	**23360**	**57109**	**111517**	**106636**	**43377**	**15949**	**11099**	**14411**	**8585**	**10835**	**13760**
External Finance											
Shareholders											
Issue of Ordinary Share Capital	-4500	-4500	-4500	-4500	-4500	-4500	1300	-4500	-4500	-5200	-5000
Dividends Paid	-18860	-52609	-107017	-102136	-38877	-11449	-12399	-9911	-4085	-5635	-8760
	-23360	**-57109**	**-111517**	**-106636**	**-43377**	**-15949**	**-11099**	**-14411**	**-8585**	**-10835**	**-13760**
Lenders											
Issue/Repayment of Loans	0	0	0	0	0	0	0	0	0	0	0
Interest	0	0	0	0	0	0	0	0	0	0	0
	0	**0**	**0**	**0**	**0**	**0**	**0**	**0**	**0**	**0**	**0**
Externally generated funds	**-23360**	**-57109**	**-111517**	**-106636**	**-43377**	**-15949**	**-11099**	**-14411**	**-8585**	**-10835**	**-13760**

CANNOCK CHASE COLLIERY COMPANY LTD
FUNDING 1860-1911

Financing for year to 31 December	1882	1883	1884	1885	1886	1887	1888	1889	1890	1891	1892
Internal Finance											
Operating Profit before interest and depreciation invested in	7575	1440	-1593	-2736	792	2070	8646	36561	36769	39422	16928
Stock	-647	-438	1049	1394	186	20	2201	590	-741	-1404	1297
Debtors	6272	-3748	-4041	6258	-9121	-761	1975	4647	-2941	1563	-1890
Creditors	-3555	-5159	-1253	-15008	718	-4158	-4317	8150	6135	1502	2737
Change in Working Capital	2070	-9345	-4245	-7356	-8217	-4899	-141	13387	2453	1661	2144
Cash Flow from operations invested in	5505	10785	2652	4620	9009	6969	8787	23174	34316	37761	14784
Bank & Cash	-3782	172	-3374	-13579	3906	1483	6991	16523	14964	9539	-12105
Fixed Assets	-149	-347	22044	9551	323	312	1811	-1269	-116	52	126
Free Cash	9436	10960	-16018	8648	4780	5174	-15	7920	19468	28170	26763
External Finance											
Shareholders											
Issue of Ordinary Share Capital	-4500	18000	18000	-2900	-2900	-2900	-2900	-2900	-2900	-2900	-800
Dividends Paid	-4778	-28488	-6982	-5748	-847	1027	1015	-10507	-15504	-24279	-25045
	-9278	**-10488**	**11018**	**-8648**	**-3747**	**-1873**	**-1885**	**-13407**	**-18404**	**-27179**	**-25845**
Lenders											
Issue/Repayment of Loans	0	0	5000	0	0	-2439	3000	6439	0	0	0
Interest	-158	-472		0	-1033	-862	-1100	-952	-1064	-991	-918
	-158	**-472**	**5000**	**0**	**-1033**	**-3301**	**1900**	**5487**	**-1064**	**-991**	**-918**
Externally generated funds	**-9436**	**-10960**	**16018**	**-8648**	**-4780**	**-5174**	**15**	**-7920**	**-19468**	**-28170**	**-26763**

CANNOCK CHASE COLLIERY COMPANY LTD
FUNDING 1860-1911

Financing for year to 31 December	1893	1894	1895	1896	1897	1898	1899	1900	1901	1902	1903
Internal Finance											
Operating Profit before interest and depreciation	-1660	8197	-3177	-6583	4779	11813	40378	115990	47825	21894	-3137
invested in											
Stock	-4003	4207	-2338	-13422	-2395	-11690	499	6450	8594	32353	1262
Debtors	-15357	-3483	1722	-427	-1727	5720	7289	269	-7081	-3586	-11563
Creditors	12353	-1594	811	-3266	3280	-2931	-1744	-2698	8583	3494	2793
Change in Working Capital	-7007	-870	195	-17115	-842	-8901	6044	4021	10096	32261	-7508
Cash Flow from operations	5347	9067	-3372	10532	5621	20714	34334	111969	37729	-10367	4371
invested in											
Bank & Cash	-3841	651	-7689	-674	-1842	3894	16540	42668	-31149	-6306	-20138
Fixed Assets	1030	1112	724	10626	6883	11165	-200	20763	20843	-41561	-724
Free Cash	8158	7304	3593	580	580	5655	17994	48538	48035	37500	25233
External Finance											
Shareholders											
Issue of Ordinary Share Capital	-800	-800	-800	0	0	0	0	0	0	0	0
Dividends Paid	-6513	-5738	-2100	0	0	-5075	-15950	-47938	-37500	-37500	-25233
	-7313	-6538	-2900	0	0	-5075	-15950	-47938	-37500	-37500	-25233
Lenders											
Issue/Repayment of Loans	0	0	0	0	0	0	-1500	-100	-10400	0	0
Interest	-845	-766	-693	-580	-580	-580	-544	-500	-135	0	0
	-845	-766	-693	-580	-580	-580	-2044	-600	-10535	0	0
Externally generated funds	-8158	-7304	-3593	-580	-580	-5655	-17994	-48538	-48035	-37500	-25233

CANNOCK CHASE COLLIERY COMPANY LTD
FUNDING 1860-1911

Financing for year to 31 December	1904	1905	1906	1907	1908	1909	1910	1911
Internal Finance								
Operating Profit before interest and depreciation	**663**	**8734**	**14062**	**54789**	**12032**	**23932**	**7299**	**22645**
invested in								
Stock	-2625	-1337	28	1012	1466	11120	2009	-1839
Debtors	2531	1883	2220	8429	-5101	-2940	5908	-1851
Creditors	-481	-1470	-942	2671	-8344	9949	-1143	-1068
Change in Working Capital	**-575**	**-924**	**1306**	**12112**	**-11979**	**18129**	**6774**	**-4758**
Cash Flow from operations	**1238**	**9658**	**12756**	**42677**	**24011**	**5803**	**525**	**27403**
invested in								
Bank & Cash	683	5795	6252	-1498	-4230	-13832	-1042	16232
Fixed Assets	555	1613	504	17925	10241	10635	-4433	2171
Free Cash	**0**	**2250**	**6000**	**26250**	**18000**	**9000**	**6000**	**9000**
External Finance								
Shareholders								
Issue of Ordinary Share Capital	0	0	0	0	0	0	0	0
Dividends Paid	0	-2250	-6000	-26250	-18000	-9000	-6000	-9000
	0	**-2250**	**-6000**	**-26250**	**-18000**	**-9000**	**-6000**	**-9000**
Lenders								
Issue/Repayment of Loans	0	0	0	0	0	0	0	0
Interest	0	0	0	0	0	0	0	0
	0	**0**	**0**	**0**	**0**	**0**	**0**	**0**
Externally generated funds	**0**	**-2250**	**-6000**	**-26250**	**-18000**	**-9000**	**-6000**	**-9000**

CANNOCK CHASE COLLIERY COMPANY LTD
FUNDING 1860-1911

Financing for year to 31 December	Summary 1860-1889	percentage 1860-1889	Summary 1890-1911	percentage 1890-1911	Summary 1860-1911	percentage 1860-1911
Internal Finance						
Operating Profit before interest and depreciation	915685	157.53	473594	133.76	1376506	149.20
invested in						
Stock	26839	4.62	28503	8.05	55342	6.00
Debtors	52342	9.00	-20413	-5.77	31929	3.46
Creditors	-47885	-8.24	28627	8.09	-19258	-2.09
Change in Working Capital	31296	5.38	36717	10.37	68013	7.37
Cash Flow from operations	884389	152.15	436877	123.39	1308493	141.83
invested in						
Bank & Cash	-2449	-0.42	12872	3.64	10423	1.13
Fixed Assets	305574	52.57	69934	19.75	375508	40.70
Free Cash	581264	100.00	354071	100.00	922562	100.00
External Finance						
Shareholders						
Issue of Ordinary Share Capital	141900	24.41	-9000	-2.54	132900	14.41
Dividends Paid	-717814	-123.49	-324875	-91.75	-1042689	-113.02
	-575914	-99.08	-333875	-94.30	-909789	-98.62
Lenders						
Issue/Repayment of Loans	12000	2.06	-12000	-3.39	0	0.00
Interest	-17350	-2.98	-8196	-2.31	-12773	-1.38
	-5350	-0.92	-20196	-5.70	-12773	-1.38
Externally generated funds	-581264	-100.00	-354071	-100.00	-922562	-100.00

CARLTON MAIN COLLIERY COMPANY LTD
FUNDING 1878-1913

Incorporated 1872 as The Yorkshire and Derbyshire Coal and Iron Company. Renamed 1900.

Financing for year to 30 June	1878	1879	1880	1881	1882	1883	1884	1885	1886	1887
Internal Finance										
Operating Profit before interest and depreciation	**385**	**-262**	**3066**	**5531**	**5860**	**11232**	**14355**	**15020**	**13890**	**19913**
invested in										
Stock	6262	58	3684	-1347	-320	-222	-68	-248	-68	-180
Debtors	16376	4061	-2194	-6447	-1585	199	1132	2886	569	1792
Creditors	-14213	-2601	4114	11	902	2361	-300	-1406	-487	-2243
Change in Working Capital	**8425**	**1518**	**5604**	**-7783**	**-1003**	**2338**	**764**	**1232**	**14**	**-631**
Cash Flow from operations	**-8040**	**-1780**	**-2538**	**13314**	**6863**	**8894**	**13591**	**13788**	**13876**	**20544**
invested in										
Cash & Bank	-24299	-1508	922	-1941	2097	5431	8328	1880	2681	10990
Fixed Assets	118345	14130	3249	10899	1201	1200	3786	3474	-377	1201
Free Cash	**-102086**	**-14402**	**-6709**	**4356**	**3565**	**2263**	**1477**	**8434**	**11572**	**8353**
External Finance										
Shareholders										
Issue of Ordinary Share Capital	68072	14539	7546	4000	4002	5281	5760	59	-5	-1
Dividends Paid		0	0	0	0	0	-6848	-7100	-7200	-7200
	68072	**14539**	**7546**	**4000**	**4002**	**5281**	**-1088**	**-7041**	**-7205**	**-7201**
Lenders										
Issue/Repayment of Loans	34014	-137	1842	-6137	-5782	-6226	1004	0	-3215	0
Interest (estimated as 7.5% pre 1896, 4.5% after)			-2679	-2219	-1785	-1318	-1393	-1393	-1152	-1152
	34014	**-137**	**-837**	**-8356**	**-7567**	**-7544**	**-389**	**-1393**	**-4367**	**-1152**
Externally generated funds	**102086**	**14402**	**6709**	**-4356**	**-3565**	**-2263**	**-1477**	**-8434**	**-11572**	**-8353**

CARLTON MAIN COLLIERY COMPANY LTD
FUNDING 1878-1913

Financing for year to 30 June	1888	1889	1890	1891	1892	1893	1894	1895	1896	1897
Internal Finance										
Operating Profit before interest and depreciation	23043	31476	60069	69866	46952	40028	26088	29373	23614	32710
invested in										
Stock	-1027	1902	1425	368	-829	289	-2089	300	470	-312
Debtors	2597	-875	791	5229	-2220	1662	3271	-625	-473	4898
Creditors	-1095	179	-564	1104	-1470	2213	1017	-2643	765	-1419
Change in Working Capital	475	1206	1652	6701	-4519	4164	2199	-2968	762	3167
Cash Flow from operations	22568	30270	58417	63165	51471	35864	23889	32341	22852	29543
invested in										
Cash & Bank	-3995	7659	15220	8589	-9129	3164	-5676	4099	3639	-11890
Fixed Assets	3884	5428	6474	1176	0	0	2265	42	1813	43503
Free Cash	22679	17183	36723	53400	60600	32700	27300	28200	17400	-2070
External Finance										
Shareholders										
Issue of Ordinary Share Capital	-1253	12000	0	0	0	0	0	0	0	0
Dividends Paid	-10800	-28800	-31601	-53400	-60600	-32700	-27300	-28200	-17400	-17400
	-12053	-16800	-31601	-53400	-60600	-32700	-27300	-28200	-17400	-17400
Lenders										
Issue/Repayment of Loans	-10242	1	-5122						0	20387
Interest (estimated as 7.5% pre 1896, 4.5% after)	-384	-384	0						0	-917
	-10626	-383	-5122						0	19470
Externally generated funds	-22679	-17183	-36723	-53400	-60600	-32700	-27300	-28200	-17400	2070

CARLTON MAIN COLLIERY COMPANY LTD
FUNDING 1878-1913

Financing for year to 30 June	1898	1899	1900	1901	1902	1903	1904	1905	1906	1907
Internal Finance										
Operating Profit before interest and depreciation	31842	46232	75356	159726	69601	86907	57504	40594	64215	60901
invested in										
Stock	440	-13	14155	3486	-2873	2329	9941	5460	1928	-4547
Debtors	5660	5031	35400	-2906	3676	2099	-902	2803	8738	21328
Creditors	-2656	1122	-22121	6367	6980	-15611	4050	4519	-6372	-2835
Change in Working Capital	3444	6140	27434	6947	7783	-11183	13089	12782	4294	13946
Cash Flow from operations	28398	40092	47922	152779	61818	98090	44415	27812	59921	46955
invested in										
Cash & Bank	-3710	3943	67317	-709	-48756	21847	17902	-51227	56474	-47709
Fixed Assets	4791	26497	-15106	76166	63575	75115	69189	63842	65556	40120
Free Cash	27317	9652	-4289	77322	46999	1128	-42676	15197	-62109	54544
External Finance										
Shareholders										
Issue of Ordinary Share Capital	0	6300	33700	0	17540	38992	33468	0	55097	22872
Dividends Paid	-26400	-26715	-54300	-93390	-76000	-42637	-46850	-38850	-32803	-66166
	-26400	-20415	-20600	-93390	-58460	-3645	-13382	-38850	22294	-43294
Lenders										
Issue/Repayment of Loans	0	12231	27599	19663	15765	7142	63543	32605	51065	0
Interest (estimated as 7.5% pre 1896, 4.5% after)	-917	-1468	-2710	-3595	-4304	-4625	-7485	-8952	-11250	-11250
	-917	10763	24889	16068	11461	2517	56058	23653	39815	-11250
Externally generated funds	-27317	-9652	4289	-77322	-46999	-1128	42676	-15197	62109	-54544

CARLTON MAIN COLLIERY COMPANY LTD
FUNDING 1878-1913

Financing for year to 30 June	1908	1909	1910	1911	1912	1913
Internal Finance						
Operating Profit before interest and depreciation	**139577**	**60633**	**65157**	**92213**	**116327**	**211346**
invested in						
Stock	15833	9073	-7045	-9181	-1369	8410
Debtors	3273	-5945	3284	19160	-48206	69736
Creditors	-14870	-9129	-15275	902	19072	-39377
Change in Working Capital	**4236**	**-6001**	**-19036**	**10881**	**-30503**	**38769**
Cash Flow from operations	**135341**	**66634**	**84193**	**81332**	**146830**	**172577**
invested in						
Cash & Bank	22071	-2697	-6883	25743	34616	28123
Fixed Assets	65718	17119	78088	30745	48031	64360
Free Cash	**47552**	**52212**	**12988**	**24844**	**64183**	**80094**
External Finance						
Shareholders						
Issue of Ordinary Share Capital	22031	13004	10654	11878	0	-172
Dividends Paid	-58333	-60000	-19830	-36354	-45682	-71475
	-36302	**-46996**	**-9176**	**-24476**	**-45682**	**-71647**
Lenders						
Issue/Repayment of Loans	0	6034	7438	10882	-7642	2394
Interest (estimated as 7.5% pre 1896, 4.5% after)	-11250	-11250	-11250	-11250	-10859	-10841
	-11250	**-5216**	**-3812**	**-368**	**-18501**	**-8447**
Externally generated funds	**-47552**	**-52212**	**-12988**	**-24844**	**-64183**	**-80094**

CARLTON MAIN COLLIERY COMPANY LTD
FUNDING 1878-1913

Financing for year to 30 June	Summary 1878-1889	percentage 1878-1889	Summary 1890-1913	percentage 1890-1913	Summary 1878-1913	percentage 1878-1913
Internal Finance						
Operating Profit before interest and depreciation	**143510**	**331.32**	**1706830**	**258.92**	**1850340**	**300.43**
invested in						
Stock	8426	19.45	45649	6.92	54075	8.78
Debtors	18511	42.74	134762	20.44	153273	24.89
Creditors	-14778	-34.12	-86231	-13.08	-101009	-16.40
Change in Working Capital	**12159**	**28.07**	**94180**	**14.29**	**106339**	**17.27**
Cash Flow from operations	**131351**	**303.25**	**1612650**	**244.63**	**1744001**	**283.16**
invested in						
Cash & Bank	8245	19.04	124361	18.87	132606	21.53
Fixed Assets	166420	384.22	829079	125.77	995499	161.63
Free Cash	**-43314**	**-100.00**	**659210**	**100.00**	**615896**	**100.00**
External Finance						
Shareholders						
Issue of Ordinary Share Capital	120000	277.05	265364	40.25	385364	62.57
Dividends Paid	-67948	-156.87	-1064386	-161.46	-1132334	-183.85
	52052	**120.17**	**-799022**	**-121.21**	**-746970**	**-121.28**
Lenders						
Issue/Repayment of Loans	5122	11.83	263984	40.05	269106	43.69
Interest (estimated as 7.5% pre 1896, 4.5% after)	-13860	-32.00	-124172	-18.84	-138032	-22.41
	-8738	**-20.17**	**139812**	**21.21**	**131074**	**21.28**
Externally generated funds	**43314**	**100.00**	**-659210**	**-100.00**	**-615896**	**-100.00**

CARRON IRON COMPANY
FUNDING 1868-1914

Incorporated by Royal Charter 1776

Financing for year to 31 December	1868 cumulative figures to 1868	1869	1870	1871	1872	1873	1874	1875	1876	1877
Internal Finance	*balancing figure*									
Operating Profit before interest and depreciation	593304	39809	50234	69588	102125	40376	111533	51138	54304	61180
invested in										
Stock	367424	8933	-45886	-139692	-41112	-3916	11016	6560	48322	63005
Debtors	65054	1358	391	30875	-23933	9544	1165	-133	-3157	6174
Creditors	-11228	-6279	-1390	-2672	-4728	-3974	-7989	-427	-4714	-3408
Change in Working Capital	421250	4012	-46885	-111489	-69773	1654	4192	6000	40451	65771
Cash Flow from operations	172054	35797	97119	181077	171898	38722	107341	45138	13853	-4591
invested in										
Cash & Bank	24742	8195	26980	135315	-11412	17523	-59631	-57079	-56271	16476
Fixed Assets	261148	-5850	-2575	-2167	99367	16094	77747	29067	15761	-47919
Free Cash	-113836	33452	72714	47929	83943	5105	89225	73150	54363	26852
External Finance										
Shareholders										
Issue of Ordinary Share Capital	111500		0	0	0	25000	0	0	0	-4500
Dividends Paid	-22300	-39025	-50175	-50175	-83625	-70375	-62700	-54150	-48450	-45600
	89200	-39025	-50175	-50175	-83625	-45375	-62700	-54150	-48450	-50100
Lenders										
Issue/Repayment of Loans	25662	6734	-21677	2729	224	41650	-24808	-18142	-5529	24002
Interest (estimated at a minimum 4%)	-1026	-1161	-862	-483	-542	-1380	-1717	-858	-384	-754
	24636	5573	-22539	2246	-318	40270	-26525	-19000	-5913	23248
Externally generated funds	113836	-33452	-72714	-47929	-83943	-5105	-89225	-73150	-54363	-26852

CARRON IRON COMPANY
FUNDING 1868-1914

Financing for year to 31 December	1878	1879	1880	1881	1882	1883	1884	1885	1886	1887
Internal Finance										
Operating Profit before interest and depreciation invested in	**11462**	**44817**	**73708**	**76083**	**86732**	**67867**	**55743**	**52426**	**51769**	**36071**
Stock	39576	15919	-8253	-25896	-55957	-36957	2387	1297	12650	-3617
Debtors	-9689	3896	-4649	7799	5075	6532	-19501	-1634	-15362	5114
Creditors	-2747	-31565	1338	-819	432	-2756	21032	-4070	1460	220
Change in Working Capital	**27140**	**-11750**	**-11564**	**-18916**	**-50450**	**-33181**	**3918**	**-4407**	**-1252**	**1717**
Cash Flow from operations invested in	**-15678**	**56567**	**85272**	**94999**	**137182**	**101048**	**51825**	**56833**	**53021**	**34354**
Cash & Bank	-31326	22868	17639	-36964	34351	-5937	-37279	20842	-17106	-6486
Fixed Assets	41584	21789	18839	150276	17592	55575	52465	22888	48674	38567
Free Cash	**-25936**	**11910**	**48794**	**-18313**	**85239**	**51410**	**36639**	**13103**	**21453**	**2273**
External Finance										
Shareholders										
Issue of Ordinary Share Capital	0	0	0	0	0	0	0	0	0	0
Dividends Paid	-39725	-28376	-34051	-45400	-48237	-45400	-31213	-25538	-25538	-22700
	-39725	**-28376**	**-34051**	**-45400**	**-48237**	**-45400**	**-31213**	**-25538**	**-25538**	**-22700**
Lenders										
Issue/Repayment of Loans	68260	20847	-10148	69495	-30439	-57	537	18784	11031	28156
Interest (estimated at a minimum 4%)	-2599	-4381	-4595	-5782	-6563	-5953	-5963	-6349	-6946	-7729
	65661	**16466**	**-14743**	**63713**	**-37002**	**-6010**	**-5426**	**12435**	**4085**	**20427**
Externally generated funds	**25936**	**-11910**	**-48794**	**18313**	**-85239**	**-51410**	**-36639**	**-13103**	**-21453**	**-2273**

CARRON IRON COMPANY
FUNDING 1868-1914

Financing for year to 31 December	1888	1889	1890	1891	1892	1893	1894	1895	1896	1897
Internal Finance										
Operating Profit before interest and depreciation	**57464**	**87662**	**57400**	**28088**	**49222**	**66907**	**65608**	**96065**	**121612**	**115344**
invested in										
Stock	-42824	-48773	-26864	-2412	-833	11579	7965	27627	-4072	13491
Debtors	16683	19994	-5368	9567	-1816	2877	328	18456	22746	2639
Creditors	18493	7777	-5737	9736	-9677	8298	1677	-2688	-6244	-2682
Change in Working Capital	**-7648**	**-21002**	**-37969**	**16891**	**-12326**	**22754**	**9970**	**43395**	**12430**	**13448**
Cash Flow from operations	**65112**	**108664**	**95369**	**11197**	**61548**	**44153**	**55638**	**52670**	**109182**	**101896**
invested in										
Cash & Bank	22095	27083	-8243	-34173	3057	11248	3505	-13065	39784	-27595
Fixed Assets	-1571	50867	64253	45451	78490	22999	23336	36903	35488	95962
Free Cash	**44588**	**30714**	**39359**	**-81**	**-19999**	**9906**	**28797**	**28832**	**33910**	**33529**
External Finance										
Shareholders										
Issue of Ordinary Share Capital	0	0	0	0	0	0	0	0	0	0
Dividends Paid	-22700	-22700	-31212	-22700	-17025	-17024	-17024	-17025	-22700	-22700
	-22700	**-22700**	**-31212**	**-22700**	**-17025**	**-17024**	**-17024**	**-17025**	**-22700**	**-22700**
Lenders										
Issue/Repayment of Loans	-13873	-282	-429	31112	46916	18314	-215	-258	341	743
Interest (estimated at a minimum 4%)	-8015	-7732	-7718	-8331	-9892	-11196	-11558	-11549	-11551	-11572
	-21888	**-8014**	**-8147**	**22781**	**37024**	**7118**	**-11773**	**-11807**	**-11210**	**-10829**
Externally generated funds	**-44588**	**-30714**	**-39359**	**81**	**19999**	**-9906**	**-28797**	**-28832**	**-33910**	**-33529**

CARRON IRON COMPANY
FUNDING 1868-1914

Financing for year to 31 December	1898	1899	1900	1901	1902	1903	1904	1905	1906	1907
Internal Finance										
Operating Profit before interest and depreciation	**117510**	**128081**	**105757**	**74618**	**99568**	**88443**	**67320**	**112459**	**147400**	**122258**
invested in										
Stock	-8769	12290	19562	-2165	44689	16013	-14019	-29487	16254	12847
Debtors	30474	25369	-10978	-25986	-2824	-12255	-5622	26092	11417	3300
Creditors	-2125	-663	-10357	4706	4769	-5023	9870	-9150	-303	-6093
Change in Working Capital	**19580**	**36996**	**-1773**	**-23445**	**46634**	**-1265**	**-9771**	**-12545**	**27368**	**10054**
Cash Flow from operations	**97930**	**91085**	**107530**	**98063**	**52934**	**89708**	**77091**	**125004**	**120032**	**112204**
invested in										
Cash & Bank	-3602	7156	4310	2631	-10910	11975	16166	3281	-21207	-14513
Fixed Assets	60400	37661	45158	47046	34243	15324	14245	77298	94917	71063
Free Cash	**41132**	**46268**	**58062**	**48386**	**29601**	**62409**	**46680**	**44425**	**46322**	**55654**
External Finance										
Shareholders										
Issue of Ordinary Share Capital	0	0	0	0	0	0	0	0	0	0
Dividends Paid	-28375	-34050	-45400	-36888	-31213	-36888	-28375	-34050	-45400	-45400
	-28375	**-34050**	**-45400**	**-36888**	**-31213**	**-36888**	**-28375**	**-34050**	**-45400**	**-45400**
Lenders										
Issue/Repayment of Loans	-1194	-692	-1174	-34	13342	-13800	-7000	806	10485	1391
Interest (estimated at a minimum 4%)	-11563	-11526	-11488	-11464	-11730	-11721	-11305	-11181	-11407	-11645
	-12757	**-12218**	**-12662**	**-11498**	**1612**	**-25521**	**-18305**	**-10375**	**-922**	**-10254**
Externally generated funds	**-41132**	**-46268**	**-58062**	**-48386**	**-29601**	**-62409**	**-46680**	**-44425**	**-46322**	**-55654**

CARRON IRON COMPANY
FUNDING 1868-1914

Financing for year to 31 December	1908	1909	1910	1911	1912	1913	1914
Internal Finance							
Operating Profit before interest and depreciation	82682	68805	102307	81324	123970	60125	64522
invested in							
Stock	-17878	28548	20159	-845	-59068	33975	3292
Debtors	-16472	-1467	33143	29125	17258	-15043	-4271
Creditors	6791	-13287	-11421	-11125	8409	-8530	15600
Change in Working Capital	**-27559**	**13794**	**41881**	**17155**	**-33401**	**10402**	**14621**
Cash Flow from operations	**110241**	**55011**	**60426**	**64169**	**157371**	**49723**	**49901**
invested in							
Cash & Bank	41252	-49471	1938	-2285	40779	4718	-5937
Fixed Assets	17479	75855	15904	34951	63468	-6395	20957
Free Cash	**51510**	**28627**	**42584**	**31503**	**53124**	**51400**	**34881**
External Finance							
Shareholders							
Issue of Ordinary Share Capital	0	0	0	0	0	0	0
Dividends Paid	-36888	-28375	-22700	-25538	-22700	-45400	-31213
	-36888	**-28375**	**-22700**	**-25538**	**-22700**	**-45400**	**-31213**
Lenders							
Issue/Repayment of Loans	-3010	11531	-8031	5844	-18876	5276	7871
Interest (estimated at a minimum 4%)	-11612	-11783	-11853	-11809	-11548	-11276	-11539
	-14622	**-252**	**-19884**	**-5965**	**-30424**	**-6000**	**-3668**
Externally generated funds	**-51510**	**-28627**	**-42584**	**-31503**	**-53124**	**-51400**	**-34881**

CARRON IRON COMPANY
FUNDING 1868-1914

Financing for year to 31 December	Summary 1869-1889	percentage 1869-1889	Summary 1890-1914	percentage 1890-1914	Summary 1869-1914	percentage 1869-1914
Internal Finance						
Operating Profit before interest and depreciation invested in	1282092	181.12	2247396.5	347.35	3529488.74	260.51
Stock	-243218	-34.36	101879	15.75	-141339	-10.43
Debtors	36542	5.16	130689	20.20	167231	12.34
Creditors	-26786	-3.78	-35249	-5.45	-62035	-4.58
Change in Working Capital	-233462	-32.98	197319	30.50	-36143	-2.67
Cash Flow from operations invested in	1515554	192.18	2050078	221.19	3565632	207.86
Cash & Bank	29876	3.79	799	0.09	30675	1.79
Fixed Assets	697070	88.39	1122456	121.11	1819526	106.07
Free Cash	788608	100.00	926823	100.00	1715431	100.00
External Finance						
Shareholders						
Issue of Ordinary Share Capital	20500	2.60	0	0.00	20500	1.20
Dividends Paid	-895853	-113.60	-746263	-80.52	-1642116	-95.73
	-875353	-111.00	-746263	-80.52	-1621616	-94.53
Lenders						
Issue/Repayment of Loans	167494	21.24	99259	10.71	266753	15.55
Interest (estimated at a minimum 4%)	-80749	-10.24	-279819	-30.19	-360568	-21.02
	86745	11.00	-180560	-19.48	-93815	-5.47
Externally generated funds	-788608	-100.00	-926823	-100.00	-1715431	-100.00

CONSETT COAL AND IRON COMPANY LTD
FUNDING 1865-1914

Financing for year to 30 June	Incorporated 1864 1864	1865	1866	1867	1868	1869	1870	1871	1872	1873	1874
Internal Finance											
Operating Profit before interest and depreciation	**15874**	**32234**	**37993**	**24879**	**25507**	**39274**	**104495**	**104019**	**163030**	**240112**	**306820**
invested in											
Stock	91604	10383	-6774	18882	4378	-15852	-13027	4393	9272	41321	-33254
Debtors	39899	-1248	19551	-8823	-11716	9960	14690	13569	19723	16035	11308
Creditors	-44690	1178	2532	-11054	8598	14719	-15973	-10169	8967	-72019	18584
Change in Working Capital	**86813**	**10313**	**15309**	**-995**	**1260**	**8827**	**-14310**	**7793**	**37962**	**-14663**	**-3362**
Cash Flow from operations	**-70939**	**21921**	**22684**	**25874**	**24247**	**30447**	**118805**	**96226**	**125068**	**254775**	**310182**
invested in											
Cash & Bank	225766	-219076	1234	14816	-1597	-10848	69776	-15654	19562	110795	-21924
Fixed Assets	265318	2100	-12418	46953	19679	19802	18003	47677	53371	62805	60453
Free Cash	**-562023**	**238897**	**33868**	**-35895**	**6165**	**21493**	**31026**	**64203**	**52135**	**81175**	**271653**
External Finance											
Shareholders											
Issue of Ordinary Share Capital	222342	84005	453	36152	9480	300	48	112	141	17	15
Dividends Paid	0	-27901	-31000	-22562	-28642	-21658	-34500	-59416	-46000	-73600	-248400
	222342	**56104**	**-30547**	**13590**	**-19162**	**-21358**	**-34452**	**-59304**	**-45859**	**-73583**	**-248385**
Lenders											
Issue/Repayment of Loans	341166	-292826	-1200	24286	15056	2098	6131	-2089	-3439	-4784	-20576
Interest (estimated at 4.5% before 1881)	-1485	-2175	-2121	-1981	-2059	-2233	-2705	-2810	-2837	-2808	-2692
	339681	**-295001**	**-3321**	**22305**	**12997**	**-135**	**3426**	**-4899**	**-6276**	**-7592**	**-23268**
Externally generated funds	**562023**	**-238897**	**-33868**	**35895**	**-6165**	**-21493**	**-31026**	**-64203**	**-52135**	**-81175**	**-271653**

CONSETT COAL AND IRON COMPANY LTD
FUNDING 1865-1914

Financing for year to 30 June	1875	1876	1877	1878	1879	1880	1881	1882	1883	1884	1885
Internal Finance											
Operating Profit before interest and depreciation	217799	89061	89101	64785	58153	110764	191677	144055	135644	89069	67980
invested in											
Stock	2061	9994	-28197	279	10310	15374	18392	4018	26731	-15527	-9159
Debtors	-24203	-30194	2614	-10212	-16487	41358	-20736	20210	-18502	-17095	6153
Creditors	9715	8203	21863	526	19018	-30879	-6211	-8477	3675	18369	-1752
Change in Working Capital	-12427	-11997	-3720	-9407	12841	25853	-8555	15751	11904	-14253	-4758
Cash Flow from operations	230226	101058	92821	74192	45312	84911	200232	128304	123740	103322	72738
invested in											
Cash & Bank	-29493	-110867	10798	10996	-9465	22393	37967	-76166	-20146	31678	-24019
Fixed Assets	62002	78440	80930	22902	4069	-11669	36102	23364	62069	26721	38017
Free Cash	197717	133485	1093	40294	50708	74187	126163	181106	81817	44923	58740
External Finance											
Shareholders											
Issue of Ordinary Share Capital	80	0	0	0	0	167	43	-8355	0	0	0
Dividends Paid	-193200	-131100	-62100	-55200	-51750	-48300	-117300	-138000	-110400	-86480	-60720
	-193120	-131100	-62100	-55200	-51750	-48133	-117257	-146355	-110400	-86480	-60720
Lenders											
Issue/Repayment of Loans	-1900	420	66819	21695	8200	-19787	-2300	-29190	34008	48425	9837
Interest (estimated at 4.5% before 1881)	-2697	-2805	-5812	-6789	-7158	-6267	-6606	-5561	-5425	-6868	-7857
	-4597	-2385	61007	14906	1042	-26054	-8906	-34751	28583	41557	1980
Externally generated funds	-197717	-133485	-1093	-40294	-50708	-74187	-126163	-181106	-81817	-44923	-58740

CONSETT COAL AND IRON COMPANY LTD
FUNDING 1865-1914

Financing for year to 30 June	1886	1887	1888	1889	1890	1891	1892	1893	1894	1895	1896
Internal Finance											
Operating Profit before interest and depreciation	**81141**	**104302**	**126198**	**228735**	**375356**	**327054**	**159218**	**123568**	**126679**	**118321**	**186445**
invested in											
Stock	13841	24644	16712	21632	25339	13645	-42350	39626	-19084	11235	-54531
Debtors	2129	2706	5324	22687	10035	4792	-37525	27341	6378	-22510	30431
Creditors	2376	-7286	-3794	-4968	-42022	9589	33576	-16657	1708	10475	-4595
Change in Working Capital	**18346**	**20064**	**18242**	**39351**	**-6648**	**28026**	**-46299**	**50310**	**-10998**	**-800**	**-28695**
Cash Flow from operations	**62795**	**84238**	**107956**	**189384**	**382004**	**299028**	**205517**	**73258**	**137677**	**119121**	**215140**
invested in											
Cash & Bank	3754	-1714	-6528	96967	52794	15748	-118287	-39789	53052	19644	84422
Fixed Assets	9452	57230	71234	17311	205266	148786	153501	153121	61099	21695	28956
Free Cash	**49589**	**28722**	**43250**	**75106**	**123944**	**134494**	**170303**	**-40074**	**23526**	**77782**	**101762**
External Finance											
Shareholders											
Issue of Ordinary Share Capital	0	36800	36799	36801	36798	193850	200000	150000	50000	0	0
Dividends Paid	-55200	-56172	-67467	-94760	-156297	-262772	-222893	-119584	-112083	-110000	-115000
	-55200	**-19372**	**-30668**	**-57959**	**-119499**	**-68922**	**-22893**	**30416**	**-62083**	**-110000**	**-115000**
Lenders											
Issue/Repayment of Loans	14250	-800	-4130	-8801	4501	-57255	-145815	9700	40450	35565	17300
Interest (estimated at 4.5% before 1881)	-8639	-8550	-8452	-8346	-8946	-8317	-1595	-42	-1893	-3347	-4062
	5611	**-9350**	**-12582**	**-17147**	**-4445**	**-65572**	**-147410**	**9658**	**38557**	**32218**	**13238**
Externally generated funds	**-49589**	**-28722**	**-43250**	**-75106**	**-123944**	**-134494**	**-170303**	**40074**	**-23526**	**-77782**	**-101762**

CONSETT COAL AND IRON COMPANY LTD
FUNDING 1865-1914

Financing for year to 30 June	1897	1898	1899	1900	1901	1902	1903	1904	1905	1906	1907
Internal Finance											
Operating Profit before interest and depreciation	**250750**	**276082**	**435314**	**672585**	**575088**	**299996**	**231324**	**250067**	**244825**	**303181**	**498468**
invested in											
Stock	53660	-19804	-31036	46644	40498	-23227	-39214	-7074	-11562	-13372	12090
Debtors	45254	32772	-4369	-3090	-35311	-18797	72806	-22325	-17072	1223	38991
Creditors	-21215	-15062	17163	-33162	24443	5235	-2605	-23538	-7369	-1986	-13899
Change in Working Capital	**77699**	**-2094**	**-18242**	**10392**	**29630**	**-36789**	**30987**	**-52937**	**-36003**	**-14135**	**37182**
Cash Flow from operations	**173051**	**278176**	**453556**	**662193**	**545458**	**336785**	**200337**	**303004**	**280828**	**317316**	**461286**
invested in											
Cash & Bank	-28369	46011	80549	339202	-338564	-116237	-55540	15704	-23440	3265	117189
Fixed Assets	52442	38728	62878	12991	465462	63022	3377	59800	76768	86551	85347
Free Cash	**148978**	**193437**	**310129**	**310000**	**418560**	**390000**	**252500**	**227500**	**227500**	**227500**	**258750**
External Finance											
Shareholders											
Issue of Ordinary Share Capital	0	0	0	0	0	0	0	0	0	0	0
Dividends Paid	-145000	-190000	-207500	-310000	-415000	-390000	-252500	-227500	-227500	-227500	-258750
	-145000	**-190000**	**-207500**	**-310000**	**-415000**	**-390000**	**-252500**	**-227500**	**-227500**	**-227500**	**-258750**
Lenders											
Issue/Repayment of Loans	0	-240	-101215	0	-3560	0	0	0	0	0	0
Interest (estimated at 4.5% before 1881)	-3978	-3197	-1414	0							
	-3978	**-3437**	**-102629**	**0**	**-3560**	**0**	**0**	**0**	**0**	**0**	**0**
Externally generated funds	**-148978**	**-193437**	**-310129**	**-310000**	**-418560**	**-390000**	**-252500**	**-227500**	**-227500**	**-227500**	**-258750**

CONSETT COAL AND IRON COMPANY LTD
FUNDING 1865-1914

Financing for year to 30 June	1908	1909	1910	1911	1912	1913	1914
Internal Finance							
Operating Profit before interest and depreciation invested in	**374019**	**243579**	**221326**	**338501**	**510558**	**585455**	**408458**
Stock	48623	-13085	-16779	62659	-58211	-38616	21706
Debtors	-69415	35992	50339	-8171	35618	-22609	-59032
Creditors	9990	-6595	-3206	4848	-35738	-5966	-21951
Change in Working Capital	**-10802**	**16312**	**30354**	**59336**	**-58331**	**-67191**	**-59277**
Cash Flow from operations	**384821**	**227267**	**190972**	**279165**	**568889**	**652646**	**467735**
invested in							
Cash & Bank	-19858	-73941	31899	42118	119507	204470	-65512
Fixed Assets	64679	23708	-18427	3297	134382	45676	68247
Free Cash	**340000**	**277500**	**177500**	**233750**	**315000**	**402500**	**465000**
External Finance							
Shareholders							
Issue of Ordinary Share Capital	0	0	0	0	0	0	0
Dividends Paid	-340000	-277500	-177500	-233750	-315000	-402500	-465000
	-340000	**-277500**	**-177500**	**-233750**	**-315000**	**-402500**	**-465000**
Lenders							
Issue/Repayment of Loans	0	0	0	0	0	0	0
Interest (estimated at 4.5% before 1881)	0	0	0	0	0	0	0
	0	**0**	**0**	**0**	**0**	**0**	**0**
Externally generated funds	**-340000**	**-277500**	**-177500**	**-233750**	**-315000**	**-402500**	**-465000**

CONSETT COAL AND IRON COMPANY LTD
FUNDING 1865-1914

Financing for year to 30 June	Summary 1864-1889	percentage 1864-1889	Summary 1890-1914	percentage 1890-1914	Summary 1864-1914	percentage 1864-1914
Internal Finance						
Operating Profit before interest and depreciation	2892702	208.17	8136217	141.06	11028918.85	154.09
invested in						
Stock	222431	16.01	-12220	-0.21	210211	2.94
Debtors	88700	6.38	71746	1.24	160446	2.24
Creditors	-78949	-5.68	-138539	-2.40	-217488	-3.04
Change in Working Capital	232182	16.71	-79013	-1.37	153169	2.14
Cash Flow from operations	2660520	191.46	8215230	142.43	10875750	151.95
invested in						
Cash & Bank	109005	7.84	346037	6.00	455042	6.36
Fixed Assets	1161917	83.62	2101352	36.43	3263269	45.59
Free Cash	1389598	100.00	5767841	100.00	7157439	100.00
External Finance						
Shareholders						
Issue of Ordinary Share Capital	455400	32.77	630648	10.93	1086048	15.17
Dividends Paid	-1921828	-138.30	-6161129	-106.82	-8082957	-112.93
	-1466428	-105.53	-5530481	-95.88	-6996909	-97.76
Lenders						
Issue/Repayment of Loans	200569	14.43	-200569	-3.48	0	0.00
Interest (estimated at 4.5% before 1881)	-123739	-8.90	-36791	-0.64	-160530	-2.24
	76830	5.53	-237360	-4.12	-160530	-2.24
Externally generated funds	-1389598	-100.00	-5767841	-100.00	-7157439	-100.00

D. DAVIS AND SON LTD
FUNDING 1890-1914

	Incorporated 1890 1890 19 months									
Financing for period to 31 May Financing for year to 31 December	1891	1892	1893	1894	1895	1896	1897	1898	1899	
Internal Finance										
Operating Profit before interest and depreciation	94336	133119	65374	45983	72560	42128	14990	25773	-3486	136562
invested in										
Stock	10000	1950	-952	-420	5251	2728	-2249	906	-2321	-859
Debtors	63680	-20479	15603	733	3787	2857	4263	-14451	-1782	11247
Creditors	-71515	1560	-6338	-2447	-97836	-47488	138694	-4898	-9829	14268
Change in Working Capital	2165	-16969	8313	-2134	-88798	-41903	140708	-18443	-13932	24656
Cash Flow from operations	92171	150088	57061	48117	161358	84031	-125718	44216	10446	111906
invested in										
Cash & Bank	135955	39799	-70750	-22921	-68252	10899	12970	-30878	-5645	28221
Fixed Assets	619966	1641	936	6413	324660	22107	5912	6646	2691	2410
Free Cash	-663750	108648	126875	64625	-95050	51025	-144600	68448	13400	81275
External Finance										
Shareholders										
Issue of Ordinary Share Capital	450000	0	0	0	0	0	100000	0	0	0
Dividends Paid	0	-48648	-45000	-45000	-45000	-39375	-16875	-14048	0	-28875
	450000	-48648	-45000	-45000	-45000	-39375	83125	-14048	0	-28875
Lenders										
Issue/Repayment of Loans	225000	-50000	-75000	-15000	148000	0	75000	-40000	0	-40000
Interest (estimated at 5% pre 1900 - see Articles)	-11250	-10000	-6875	-4625	-7950	-11650	-13525	-14400	-13400	-12400
	213750	-60000	-81875	-19625	140050	-11650	61475	-54400	-13400	-52400
Externally generated funds	663750	-108648	-126875	-64625	95050	-51025	144600	-68448	-13400	-81275

D. DAVIS AND SON LTD
FUNDING 1890-1914

Financing for period to 31 May Financing for year to 31 December	1900	1901	1902	1903	1904	1905	1906	1907	1908	1909
Internal Finance										
Operating Profit before interest and depreciation	**114723**	**138920**	**129361**	**62775**	**65742**	**60647**	**169236**	**225619**	**168724**	**90685**
invested in										
Stock	4191	-2998	7129	-2558	-4000	2692	11008	-1708	8846	-5249
Debtors	-9393	5040	8899	15366	-18957	-8184	39021	-7485	-7474	4459
Creditors	11906	-3390	-7561	4965	10160	2876	-26469	-873	-15549	-23255
Change in Working Capital	**6704**	**-1348**	**8467**	**17773**	**-12797**	**-2616**	**23560**	**-10066**	**-14177**	**-24045**
Cash Flow from operations	**108019**	**140268**	**120894**	**45002**	**78539**	**63263**	**145676**	**235685**	**182901**	**114730**
invested in										
Cash & Bank	3289	29970	54646	-53669	11114	-12020	44182	-75742	36949	6584
Fixed Assets	33877	10749	2479	3763	6956	21427	45734	163396	82878	50773
Free Cash	**70853**	**99549**	**63769**	**94908**	**60469**	**53856**	**55760**	**147431**	**63074**	**57373**
External Finance										
Shareholders										
Issue of Ordinary Share Capital	0	0	0	0	0	0	0	0	0	0
Dividends Paid	-51000	-51000	-51000	-51000	-51000	-39750	-39750	-51000	-51000	-45375
	-51000	**-51000**	**-51000**	**-51000**	**-51000**	**-39750**	**-39750**	**-51000**	**-51000**	**-45375**
Lenders										
Issue/Repayment of Loans	0	-34000	0	-34000	0	-3400	0	-81600	0	0
Interest (estimated at 5%	-19853	-14549	-12769	-9908	-9469	-10706	-16010	-14831	-12074	-11998
pre 1900 - see Articles)	**-19853**	**-48549**	**-12769**	**-43908**	**-9469**	**-14106**	**-16010**	**-96431**	**-12074**	**-11998**
Externally generated funds	**-70853**	**-99549**	**-63769**	**-94908**	**-60469**	**-53856**	**-55760**	**-147431**	**-63074**	**-57373**

D. DAVIS AND SON LTD
FUNDING 1890-1914

Financing for period to 31 May Financing for year to 31 December	1910	1911	1912	1913	1914	Summary 1890-1914	percentages 1890-1914
Internal Finance							
Operating Profit before interest and depreciation	**174921**	**158769**	**148960**	**221720**	**219494**	**2777635**	**469.72**
invested in							
Stock	-2534	8698	12681	6042	-6861	49413	8.36
Debtors	17327	3585	23750	40172	111555	283139	47.88
Creditors	4350	-9303	-94218	17004	35204	-179982	-30.44
Change in Working Capital	**19143**	**2980**	**-57787**	**63218**	**139898**	**152570**	**25.80**
Cash Flow from operations	**155778**	**155789**	**206747**	**158502**	**79596**	**2625065**	**443.92**
invested in							
Cash & Bank	59828	-93559	20235	42336	-75666	27875	4.71
Fixed Assets	35575	354598	82970	160963	-44267	2005853	339.21
Free Cash	**60375**	**-105250**	**103542**	**-44797**	**199529**	**591337**	**100.00**
External Finance							
Shareholders							
Issue of Ordinary Share Capital	0	0	40955	34088	37457	662500	112.03
Dividends Paid	-56625	-51000	-56997	-85541	-106986	-1121845	-189.71
	-56625	**-51000**	**-16042**	**-51453**	**-69529**	**-459345**	**-77.68**
Lenders							
Issue/Repayment of Loans	0	160000	-83750	100000	-126250	125000	21.14
Interest (estimated at 5%	-3750	-3750	-3750	-3750	-3750	-256992	-43.46
pre 1900 - see Articles)	**-3750**	**156250**	**-87500**	**96250**	**-130000**	**-131992**	**-22.32**
Externally generated funds	**-60375**	**105250**	**-103542**	**44797**	**-199529**	**-591337**	**-100.00**

DOWLAIS IRON (PARTNERSHIP)
FUNDING 1865-1884

| | Incorporated 1898 | | | | | | | | | | | |
Financing to 31 March	1865 cumulative figures to 1865	1866	1867	1868	1869	1870	1871	1872	1873	1874	1875	1876
Internal Finance												
balancing figure												
Operating Profit before interest and depreciation	141178	105475	108015	96132	116587	215597	200105	272359	238385	317530	91710	84787
invested in												
Stock	227492	-1213	-61571	70408	143759	0	-111405	129322	-26765	87556	-191320	152417
Debtors	153595	23614	147160	-2342	-80119	0	162924	52054	26251	68688	15874	-142076
Creditors	-46668	-1381	-3068	-12752	-1756	-1	1911	-22308	28414	-32565	31892	-15026
Change in Working Capital	334419	21020	82521	55314	61884	-1	53430	159068	27900	123679	-143554	-4685
Cash Flow from operations	-193241	84455	25494	40818	54703	215598	146675	113291	210485	193851	235264	89472
invested in												
Cash & Bank	1262	509	-384	-188	457	0	1007	-441	-49	2315	-3562	114
Fixed Assets	308697	42972	11278	5591	7551	17841	34265	22523	53986	67056	57060	44699
Free Cash	-503200	40974	14600	35415	46695	197757	111403	91209	156548	124480	181766	44659
External Finance												
Shareholders												
Partnership Capital	503200	0	0	0	0	0	0	0	0	0	0	0
Profits Distributed	0	-40974	-14600	-35415	-46695	-197757	-111403	-91209	-156548	-124480	-181766	-44659
	503200	-40974	-14600	-35415	-46695	-197757	-111403	-91209	-156548	-124480	-181766	-44659
Lenders												
Issue/Repayment of Loans	0	0	0	0	0	0	0	0	0	0	0	0
Interest	0	0	0	0	0	0	0	0	0	0	0	0
	0	0	0	0	0	0	0	0	0	0	0	0
Externally generated funds	503200	-40974	-14600	-35415	-46695	-197757	-111403	-91209	-156548	-124480	-181766	-44659

DOWLAIS IRON (PARTNERSHIP)
FUNDING 1865-1884

Financing to 31 March	1877	1878	1879	1880	1881	1882	1883	1884	Summary 1864-1884	percentage 1864-1884
Internal Finance										
Operating Profit before interest and depreciation	**123685**	**94985**	**128468**	**171707**	**182925**	**254424**	**163597**	**98044**	**3205695**	**333.54**
invested in										
Stock	66137	-71955	127966	-163558	5162	-99245	81977	11486	376650	39.19
Debtors	-52688	109145	-70779	286521	66837	231982	-33721	6951	969871	100.91
Creditors	5808	-2886	615	-13073	13829	-622	-21688	10345	-80980	-8.43
Change in Working Capital	**19257**	**34304**	**57802**	**109890**	**85828**	**132115**	**26568**	**28782**	**1265541**	**131.68**
Cash Flow from operations	**104428**	**60681**	**70666**	**61817**	**97097**	**122309**	**137029**	**69262**	**1940154**	**201.87**
invested in										0.00
Cash & Bank	1056	-607	-213	212	222	-506	186	262	1652	0.17
Fixed Assets	64179	22860	24477	27386	38887	61983	36837	27268	977396	101.69
Free Cash	**39193**	**38428**	**46402**	**34219**	**57988**	**60832**	**100006**	**41732**	**961106**	**100.00**
External Finance										
Shareholders										
Partnership Capital	0	0	0	0	0	0	0	0	503200	52.36
Profits Distributed	-39193	-38428	-46402	-34219	-57988	-60832	-100006	-41732	-1464306	-152.36
	-39193	**-38428**	**-46402**	**-34219**	**-57988**	**-60832**	**-100006**	**-41732**	**-961106**	**-100.00**
Lenders										
Issue/Repayment of Loans	0	0	0	0	0	0	0	0	0	0.00
Interest	0	0	0	0	0	0	0	0	0	0.00
	0	**0**	**0**	**0**	**0**	**0**	**0**	**0**	**0**	**0.00**
Externally generated funds	**-39193**	**-38428**	**-46402**	**-34219**	**-57988**	**-60832**	**-100006**	**-41732**	**-961106**	**-100.00**

EBBW VALE STEEL AND IRON COMPANY LTD
FUNDING 1881-1914

Financing for year to 31 March	1881	1882	1883	1884	1885	1886	1887	1888	1889	1890	1891	1892
	Incorporated 1864											
	cumulative figures to 1881											
Internal Finance												
	balancing figure											
Operating Profit before interest and depreciation invested in	83340	82759	74969	17897	39546	40252	18353	58416	3792	76057	98786	37353
Stock	265970	-1020	17952	-23068	-70326	-2548	-44397	20806	-18562	-17437	44159	-67507
Debtors	234031	-73078	36716	-30245	-10296	-22139	-21851	-6673	16270	3651	3455	10530
Creditors	-239971	64273	-52604	-36093	61409	2671	33504	43571	-53938	1118	-65551	-17894
Change in Working Capital	260030	-9825	2064	-89406	-19213	-22016	-32744	57704	-56230	-12668	-17937	-74871
Cash Flow from operations invested in	-176690	92584	72905	107303	58759	62268	51097	712	60022	88725	116723	112224
Cash & Bank	83051	-5552	7870	11927	-40116	4515	5853	-20816	-1454	-4011	-19205	13871
Fixed Assets	1832628	18971	36694	28438	6173	-3299	3761	3745	11943	32836	32937	46089
Free Cash	-2092369	79165	28341	66938	92702	61052	41483	17783	49533	59900	102991	52264
External Finance												
Shareholders												
Issue of Ordinary Share Capital	1503663	0	0	0	0	0	0	0	0	0	0	0
Dividends Paid		-153	-18539	-18643	0	-10	0	-3	-3	0	-26002	-43
	1503663	-153	-18539	-18643	0	-10	0	-3	-3	0	-26002	-43
Lenders												
Issue/Repayment of Loans	622700	-45700	22250	-15850	-63143	-34280	-16150	7145	-25810	-38323	-58412	-35955
Interest	-33994	-33312	-32052	-32445	-29559	-26762	-25333	-24925	-23720	-21577	-18577	-16266
	588706	-79012	-9802	-48295	-92702	-61042	-41483	-17780	-49530	-59900	-76989	-52221
Externally generated funds	2092369	-79165	-28341	-66938	-92702	-61052	-41483	-17783	-49533	-59900	-102991	-52264

EBBW VALE STEEL AND IRON COMPANY LTD
FUNDING 1881-1914

Financing for year to 31 March	1893	1894	1895	1896	1897	1898	1899	1900	1901	1902	1903	1904
Internal Finance												
Operating Profit before interest and depreciation	**84408**	**103840**	**41416**	**28031**	**69821**	**52445**	**34699**	**231695**	**199858**	**32263**	**162445**	**110955**
invested in												
Stock	-539	11283	53926	-53286	-3807	81810	-72677	30611	22063	-2020	14495	-22852
Debtors	-14188	-394	415	18449	-16985	13412	-1439	36681	11997	-14982	-14288	21410
Creditors	133273	41952	-36785	35234	22909	-124232	68601	31259	-15191	-84022	76495	1517
Change in Working Capital	**118546**	**52841**	**17556**	**397**	**2117**	**-29010**	**-5515**	**98551**	**18869**	**-101024**	**76702**	**75**
Cash Flow from operations	**-34138**	**50999**	**23860**	**27634**	**67704**	**81455**	**40214**	**133144**	**180989**	**133287**	**85743**	**110880**
invested in												
Cash & Bank	18568	3931	-53877	2122	8616	-6733	1281	66068	-53062	-4883	10600	15906
Fixed Assets	14758	16524	55676	14562	36469	37698	16312	25869	122133	26216	52530	-2066
Free Cash	**-67464**	**30544**	**22061**	**10950**	**22619**	**50490**	**22621**	**41207**	**111918**	**111954**	**22613**	**97040**
External Finance												
Shareholders												
Issue of Ordinary Share Capital	0	0	0	0	0	0	0	0	0	0	0	0
Dividends Paid	0	-41	-37230	-5	-5	-27877	-8	-18594	-89305	-89341	0	-74427
	0	**-41**	**-37230**	**-5**	**-5**	**-27877**	**-8**	**-18594**	**-89305**	**-89341**	**0**	**-74427**
Lenders												
Issue/Repayment of Loans	84278	-11250	35000	11600	0	0	0	0	0	0	0	0
Interest	-16814	-19253	-19831	-22545	-22614	-22613	-22613	-22613	-22613	-22613	-22613	-22613
	67464	**-30503**	**15169**	**-10945**	**-22614**	**-22613**	**-22613**	**-22613**	**-22613**	**-22613**	**-22613**	**-22613**
Externally generated funds	**67464**	**-30544**	**-22061**	**-10950**	**-22619**	**-50490**	**-22621**	**-41207**	**-111918**	**-111954**	**-22613**	**-97040**

EBBW VALE STEEL AND IRON COMPANY LTD
FUNDING 1881-1914

Financing for year to 31 March	1905	1906	1907	1908	1909	1910	1911	1912	1913	1914
Internal Finance										
Operating Profit before interest and depreciation	**72352**	**76280**	**155500**	**145585**	**73110**	**77328**	**45617**	**64618**	**170869**	**150701**
invested in										
Stock	943	-43862	22525	25713	22576	-24829	40471	-49541	82497	-8986
Debtors	-8721	12493	11421	-9612	-28789	33555	25314	-141785	149393	53950
Creditors	-62334	-21203	-7105	4869	-14265	-1480	-58020	141314	-250945	7967
Change in Working Capital	**-70112**	**-52572**	**26841**	**20970**	**-20478**	**7246**	**7765**	**-50012**	**-19055**	**52931**
Cash Flow from operations	**142464**	**128852**	**128659**	**124615**	**93588**	**70082**	**37852**	**114630**	**189924**	**97770**
invested in										
Cash & Bank	-799	5662	-39657	7366	-912	374	3458	-510	344	-12063
Fixed Assets	75980	63412	71715	25833	2761	30382	36145	72813	157899	189743
Free Cash	**67283**	**59778**	**96601**	**91416**	**91739**	**39326**	**-1751**	**42327**	**31681**	**-79910**
External Finance										
Shareholders										
Issue of Ordinary Share Capital	0	0	0	0	0	0	0	0	0	210937
Dividends Paid	-44670	-37165	-37316	-70708	-71031	-18618	-37238	-18619	-22343	-83785
	-44670	**-37165**	**-37316**	**-70708**	**-71031**	**-18618**	**-37238**	**-18619**	**-22343**	**127152**
Lenders										
Issue/Repayment of Loans	0	0	-38100	0	0	0	60000	0	14370	-24370
Interest	-22613	-22613	-21185	-20708	-20708	-20708	-21011	-23708	-23708	-22872
	-22613	**-22613**	**-59285**	**-20708**	**-20708**	**-20708**	**38989**	**-23708**	**-9338**	**-47242**
Externally generated funds	**-67283**	**-59778**	**-96601**	**-91416**	**-91739**	**-39326**	**1751**	**-42327**	**-31681**	**79910**

EBBW VALE STEEL AND IRON COMPANY LTD
FUNDING 1881-1914

Financing for year to 31 March	Summary 1881-1889	percentage 1881-1889	Summary 1890-1914	percentage 1890-1914	Summary 1881-1914	percentage 1881-1914
Internal Finance						
Operating Profit before interest and depreciation	419324	25.33	2396032	212.00	2815356	-536.08
invested in						
Stock	144807	8.75	85729	7.59	230536	-43.90
Debtors	122735	7.41	154943	13.71	277678	-52.87
Creditors	-177178	-10.70	-192519	-17.03	-369697	70.40
Change in Working Capital	90364	5.46	48153	4.26	138517	-26.38
Cash Flow from operations	328960	19.87	2347879	207.74	2676839	-509.71
invested in						
Cash & Bank	45278	2.74	-37545	-3.32	7733	-1.47
Fixed Assets	1939054	117.14	1255226	111.06	3194280	-608.23
Free Cash	-1655372	-100.00	1130198	100.00	-525174	100.00
External Finance						
Shareholders						
Issue of Ordinary Share Capital	1503663	90.84	210937	18.66	1714600	-326.48
Dividends Paid	-37351	-2.26	-804371	-71.17	-841722	160.27
	1466312	88.58	-593434	-52.51	872878	-166.21
Lenders						
Issue/Repayment of Loans	451162	27.25	-1162	-0.10	450000	-85.69
Interest	-262102	-15.83	-535602	-47.39	-797704	151.89
	189060	11.42	-536764	-47.49	-347704	66.21
Externally generated funds	1655372	100.00	-1130198	-100.00	525174	-100.00

GUEST, KEEN AND NETTLEFOLDS LTD
FUNDING 1901-1914

Incorporated as Guest Keen 1900. Merged with Nettlefolds 1902.

Financing for year to 30 June	1901	1902	1903	1904	1905	1906	1907	1908	1909	1910
Internal Finance										
Operating Profit before interest and depreciation	**394066**	**466984**	**441711**	**473359**	**439247**	**627989**	**535579**	**560875**	**389359**	**366306**
invested in										
Stock	352350	13521	-15151	-2222	16998	-26193	10516	55177	-8230	-20277
Debtors	344578	5559	1015	46966	-69177	90314	90560	-134443	-32922	47708
Creditors	-294437	55168	18369	-22923	-21872	-24169	-16441	28932	29139	25914
Change in Working Capital	**402491**	**74248**	**4233**	**21821**	**-74051**	**39952**	**84635**	**-50334**	**-12013**	**53345**
Cash Flow from operations	**-8425**	**392736**	**437478**	**451538**	**513298**	**588037**	**450944**	**611209**	**401372**	**312961**
invested in										
Cash & Bank	516994	-337964	-3296	22282	10293	12946	-10582	94280	-13152	-57317
Fixed Assets	1940984	480396	188572	176206	250186	322272	208707	215860	113609	69826
Free Cash	**-2466403**	**250304**	**252202**	**253050**	**252819**	**252819**	**252819**	**301069**	**300915**	**300452**
External Finance										
Shareholders										
Issue of Ordinary Share Capital	1530000	0	0	0	0	0	0	0	0	0
Dividends Paid	-32047	-196697	-182500	-182500	-182500	-182500	-182500	-230750	-230750	-230750
	1497953	**-196697**	**-182500**	**-182500**	**-182500**	**-182500**	**-182500**	**-230750**	**-230750**	**-230750**
Lenders										
Issue/Repayment of Loans	1000000	0	0	0	0	0	0	0	0	0
Interest	-31550	-53607	-69702	-70550	-70319	-70319	-70319	-70319	-70165	-69702
	968450	**-53607**	**-69702**	**-70550**	**-70319**	**-70319**	**-70319**	**-70319**	**-70165**	**-69702**
Externally generated funds	**2466403**	**-250304**	**-252202**	**-253050**	**-252819**	**-252819**	**-252819**	**-301069**	**-300915**	**-300452**

GUEST, KEEN AND NETTLEFOLDS LTD
FUNDING 1901-1914

Financing for year to 30 June	1911	1912	1913	1914	Summary 1900-1914	percentage 1900-1914
Internal Finance						
Operating Profit before interest and depreciation	**405403**	**421542**	**513090**	**451887**	**6487397**	**563.29**
invested in						
Stock	53332	-66776	15736	140655	519436	45.10
Debtors	-32321	46373	100662	-127704	377168	32.75
Creditors	-39348	-15538	-69058	16284	-329980	-28.65
Change in Working Capital	**-18337**	**-35941**	**47340**	**29235**	**566624**	**49.20**
Cash Flow from operations	**423740**	**457483**	**465750**	**422652**	**5920773**	**514.09**
invested in						
Cash & Bank	36529	54743	26763	3282	355801	30.89
Fixed Assets	86759	102288	138535	119072	4413272	383.20
Free Cash	**300452**	**300452**	**300452**	**300298**	**1151700**	**100.00**
External Finance						
Shareholders						
Issue of Ordinary Share Capital	0	0	0	0	1530000	132.85
Dividends Paid	-230750	-230750	-230750	-230750	-2756494	-239.34
	-230750	**-230750**	**-230750**	**-230750**	**-1226494**	**-106.49**
Lenders						
Issue/Repayment of Loans	0	0	0	0	1000000	86.83
Interest	-69702	-69702	-69702	-69548	-925206	-80.33
	-69702	**-69702**	**-69702**	**-69548**	**74794**	**6.49**
Externally generated funds	**-300452**	**-300452**	**-300452**	**-300298**	**-1151700**	**-100.00**

HENRY BRIGGS, SON AND COMPANY LTD
FUNDING 1865-1914

Financing for year to 30 June	1866	1867	1868	1869	1870	1871	1872	1873	1874	1875
	Incorporated 1865									
Internal Finance										
Operating Profit before interest and depreciation	**21691**	**30308**	**29377**	**30037**	**26431**	**27261**	**39372**	**70535**	**76109**	**35849**
invested in										
Stock	15641	0	0	0	3022	-2579	2385	11168	15298	714
Debtors	24668	7388	66	3200	127	-4122	13186	-1705	-7658	6130
Creditors	-16925	280	-3067	-3711	-988	-791	-2491	-12471	-4402	17245
Change in Working Capital	**23384**	**7668**	**-3001**	**-511**	**2161**	**-7492**	**13080**	**-3008**	**3238**	**24089**
Cash Flow from operations	**-1693**	**22640**	**32378**	**30548**	**24270**	**34753**	**26292**	**73543**	**72871**	**11760**
invested in										
Cash & Bank	3721	-451	4721	-663	-217	-2836	2052	53250	-49280	-2101
Fixed Assets	79934	19818	24233	21282	11092	25844	21837	27900	125439	50327
Free Cash	**-85348**	**3273**	**3424**	**9929**	**13395**	**11745**	**2403**	**-7607**	**-3288**	**-36466**
External Finance										
Shareholders										
Issue of Ordinary Share Capital	89648	352	7026	1958	546	293	9990	27905	42244	25641
Dividends Paid	-4300	-10800	-11700	-13137	-13866	-12188	-12393	-20498	-39056	-35925
	85348	**-10448**	**-4674**	**-11179**	**-13320**	**-11895**	**-2403**	**7407**	**3188**	**-10284**
Lenders										
Issue/Repayment of Loans	0	7175	1250	1250	-75	150	0	200	100	46750
Interest										
	0	**7175**	**1250**	**1250**	**-75**	**150**	**0**	**200**	**100**	**46750**
Externally generated funds	**85348**	**-3273**	**-3424**	**-9929**	**-13395**	**-11745**	**-2403**	**7607**	**3288**	**36466**

HENRY BRIGGS, SON AND COMPANY LTD
FUNDING 1865-1914

Financing for year to 30 June	1876	1877	1878	1879	1880	1881	1882	1883	1884	1885
Internal Finance										
Operating Profit before interest and depreciation invested in	**36109**	**27592**	**22690**	**21796**	**15750**	**18690**	**9209**	**14614**	**11651**	**5497**
Stock	-1390	-622	4722	-5470	-2978	2272	-1272	-4492	-502	-1429
Debtors	-4164	8518	-15333	4788	1764	-4561	-7403	6735	-10327	-1243
Creditors	1333	-7085	461	8273	4767	-530	3106	-6737	1629	6138
Change in Working Capital	**-4221**	**811**	**-10150**	**7591**	**3553**	**-2819**	**-5569**	**-4494**	**-9200**	**3466**
Cash Flow from operations invested in	**40330**	**26781**	**32840**	**14205**	**12197**	**21509**	**14778**	**19108**	**20851**	**2031**
Cash & Bank	10182	-12623	10850	-5133	-5673	5761	-4183	558	1357	-12849
Fixed Assets	23548	25934	18847	10101	1268	3743	3866	9056	6667	10319
Free Cash	**6600**	**13470**	**3143**	**9237**	**16602**	**12005**	**15095**	**9494**	**12827**	**4561**
External Finance										
Shareholders										
Issue of Ordinary Share Capital	10714	3530	9085	3348	846	402	2	0	1	0
Dividends Paid	-25314	-21900	-8795	-7618	-6475	-6475	-6475	0	-6475	0
	-14600	**-18370**	**290**	**-4270**	**-5629**	**-6073**	**-6473**	**0**	**-6474**	**0**
Lenders										
Issue/Repayment of Loans	8000	4900	600	-900	-7300	-2300	-5150	-6300	-3350	-1900
Interest			-4033	-4067	-3673	-3632	-3472	-3194	-3003	-2661
	8000	**4900**	**-3433**	**-4967**	**-10973**	**-5932**	**-8622**	**-9494**	**-6353**	**-4561**
Externally generated funds	**-6600**	**-13470**	**-3143**	**-9237**	**-16602**	**-12005**	**-15095**	**-9494**	**-12827**	**-4561**

HENRY BRIGGS, SON AND COMPANY LTD
FUNDING 1865-1914

Financing for year to 30 June	1886	1887	1888	1889	1890	1891	1892	1893	1894	1895
Internal Finance										
Operating Profit before interest and depreciation	**19845**	**22187**	**25921**	**29131**	**56963**	**94420**	**75350**	**41217**	**35565**	**32990**
invested in										
Stock	342	-1491	-1102	24	359	-2810	-592	-502	-26	-925
Debtors	3763	14310	-1616	-6932	3670	24812	-11853	-15664	8763	-8316
Creditors	-2020	3532	2126	-1245	-7831	-4097	-3031	-3238	-739	-8293
Change in Working Capital	**2085**	**16351**	**-592**	**-8153**	**-3802**	**17905**	**-15476**	**-19404**	**7998**	**-17534**
Cash Flow from operations	**17760**	**5836**	**26513**	**37284**	**60765**	**76515**	**90826**	**60621**	**27567**	**50524**
invested in										
Cash & Bank	15171	-2955	4505	-2676	17305	13305	9572	-6576	-9467	-12145
Fixed Assets	-3468	-2882	-1134	14916	9508	19366	34779	19679	9842	36473
Free Cash	**6057**	**11673**	**23142**	**25044**	**33952**	**43844**	**46475**	**47518**	**27192**	**26196**
External Finance										
Shareholders										
Issue of Ordinary Share Capital	0	12	-695	-45	0	-327	0	-3	-960	0
Dividends Paid	0	-6475	-10361	-12951	-23310	-38851	-45325	-45326	-25900	-25900
	0	**-6463**	**-11056**	**-12996**	**-23310**	**-39178**	**-45325**	**-45329**	**-26860**	**-25900**
Lenders										
Issue/Repayment of Loans	-3500	-2800	-10200	-10400	-9700	-4000	-700	-1800	0	0
Interest	-2557	-2410	-1886	-1648	-942	-666	-450	-389	-332	-296
	-6057	**-5210**	**-12086**	**-12048**	**-10642**	**-4666**	**-1150**	**-2189**	**-332**	**-296**
Externally generated funds	**-6057**	**-11673**	**-23142**	**-25044**	**-33952**	**-43844**	**-46475**	**-47518**	**-27192**	**-26196**

HENRY BRIGGS, SON AND COMPANY LTD
FUNDING 1865-1914

Financing for year to 30 June	1896	1897	1898	1899	1900	1901	1902	1903	1904	1905
Internal Finance										
Operating Profit before interest and depreciation	**26185**	**24754**	**33167**	**12029**	**102813**	**141971**	**67001**	**50546**	**61753**	**40532**
invested in										
Stock	267	4897	-45	2905	1677	-2051	-2817	3268	207	352
Debtors	3101	8547	10051	6648	6852	-14225	-10166	-1366	-2875	-4674
Creditors	5931	-13919	-885	-5465	-5573	-12798	-1368	-8855	4755	6727
Change in Working Capital	**9299**	**-475**	**9121**	**4088**	**2956**	**-29074**	**-14351**	**-6953**	**2087**	**2405**
Cash Flow from operations	**16886**	**25229**	**24046**	**7941**	**99857**	**171045**	**81352**	**57499**	**59666**	**38127**
invested in										
Cash & Bank	6549	10317	-7734	-2602	25983	15505	-14351	-8528	-5011	8465
Fixed Assets	-48383	-916	12067	22344	22453	83551	13430	9464	18399	-26900
Free Cash	**58720**	**15828**	**19713**	**-11801**	**51421**	**71989**	**82273**	**56563**	**46278**	**56562**
External Finance										
Shareholders										
Issue of Ordinary Share Capital	-156	0	0	39106	0	0	0	0	0	0
Dividends Paid	-58276	-15540	-19425	-27138	-51421	-71989	-82273	-56563	-46278	-56562
	-58432	**-15540**	**-19425**	**11968**	**-51421**	**-71989**	**-82273**	**-56563**	**-46278**	**-56562**
Lenders										
Issue/Repayment of Loans	0	0	0	0	0	0	0	0	0	0
Interest	-288	-288	-288	-167	0	0	0	0	0	0
	-288	**-288**	**-288**	**-167**	**0**	**0**	**0**	**0**	**0**	**0**
Externally generated funds	**-58720**	**-15828**	**-19713**	**11801**	**-51421**	**-71989**	**-82273**	**-56563**	**-46278**	**-56562**

HENRY BRIGGS, SON AND COMPANY LTD
FUNDING 1865-1914

Financing for year to 30 June	1906	1907	1908	1909	1910	1911	1912	1913	1914
Internal Finance									
Operating Profit before interest and depreciation invested in	**68965**	**70459**	**102223**	**57337**	**57724**	**43061**	**79071**	**124938**	**105386**
Stock	-38	5097	1050	3524	3215	1349	-4470	816	10015
Debtors	4911	17437	-4632	-10397	2059	-6101	22490	16721	3434
Creditors	-6275	-3123	3863	-1592	-18794	-8533	4557	-5306	-1308
Change in Working Capital	**-1402**	**19411**	**281**	**-8465**	**-13520**	**-13285**	**22577**	**12231**	**12141**
Cash Flow from operations	**70367**	**51048**	**101942**	**65802**	**71244**	**56346**	**56494**	**112707**	**93245**
invested in									
Cash & Bank	-13577	14923	1935	-21493	-9528	-12582	16862	21808	10398
Fixed Assets	22239	-4616	31700	35381	47984	32862	6844	36800	17272
Free Cash	**61705**	**40741**	**68307**	**51914**	**32788**	**36066**	**32788**	**54099**	**65575**
External Finance									
Shareholders									
Issue of Ordinary Share Capital	0	0	0	0	0	0	0	0	0
Dividends Paid	-61705	-40741	-68307	-51914	-32788	-36066	-32788	-54099	-65575
	-61705	**-40741**	**-68307**	**-51914**	**-32788**	**-36066**	**-32788**	**-54099**	**-65575**
Lenders									
Issue/Repayment of Loans	0	0	0	0	0	0	0	0	0
Interest	0	0	0	0	0	0	0	0	0
	0	**0**	**0**	**0**	**0**	**0**	**0**	**0**	**0**
Externally generated funds	**-61705**	**-40741**	**-68307**	**-51914**	**-32788**	**-36066**	**-32788**	**-54099**	**-65575**

HENRY BRIGGS, SON AND COMPANY LTD
FUNDING 1865-1914

Financing for year to 30 June	Summary 1865-1889	percentage 1865-1889	Summary 1890-1914	percentage 1890-1914	Summary 1865-1914	percentage 1865-1914
Internal Finance						
Operating Profit before interest and depreciation	667652	830.31	1606420	143.85	2274072	189.96
invested in						
Stock	32261	40.12	24722	2.21	56983	4.76
Debtors	29579	36.79	49227	4.41	78806	6.58
Creditors	-13573	-16.88	-95190	-8.52	-108763	-9.09
Change in Working Capital	48267	60.03	-21241	-1.90	27026	2.26
Cash Flow from operations	619385	770.28	1627661	145.76	2247046	187.70
invested in						
Cash & Bank	10488	13.04	49333	4.42	59821	5.00
Fixed Assets	528487	657.24	461622	41.34	990109	82.71
Free Cash	80410	100.00	1116706	100.00	1197116	100.00
External Finance						
Shareholders						
Issue of Ordinary Share Capital	232803	289.52	37660	3.37	270463	22.59
Dividends Paid	-293177	-364.60	-1134060	-101.55	-1427237	-119.22
	-60374	-75.08	-1096400	-98.18	-1156774	-96.63
Lenders						
Issue/Repayment of Loans	16200	20.15	-16200	-1.45	0	0.00
Interest	-36236	-45.06	-4106	-0.37	-40342	-3.37
	-20036	-24.92	-20306	-1.82	-40342	-3.37
Externally generated funds	-80410	-100.00	-1116706	-100.00	-1197116	-100.00

JOHN BROWN AND COMPANY LTD
FUNDING 1881-1914

Incorporated 1863

Financing for year to 31 March	1881	1882	1883	1884	1885	1886	1887	1888	1889	1890
	cumulative figures to 1881									
Internal Finance	balancing figure									
Operating Profit before interest and depreciation	150904	67320	68335	85424	73658	73015	86671	61178	50123	131898
invested in										
Stock	264328	-135	-6760	14589	-25189	12467	-11580	-12755	26093	83685
Debtors	163777	8672	12502	-21899	-10750	16368	22350	-54498	53709	14641
Creditors	-246582	55421	-59215	34939	38985	-54783	32194	25788	-110259	-40967
Change in Working Capital	181523	63958	-53473	27629	3046	-25948	42964	-41465	-30457	57359
Cash Flow from operations	-30619	3362	121808	57795	70612	98963	43707	102643	80580	74539
invested in										
Cash & Bank	11517	-3800	15794	-15323	-1217	-1523	17076	-7093	626	-10479
Fixed Assets	933707	46367	45298	5101	12903	29731	44141	48111	37124	23445
Free Cash	-975843	-39205	60716	68017	58926	70755	-17510	61625	42830	61573
External Finance										
Shareholders										
Issue of Ordinary Share Capital	728070	70905	4185	220	8560	3930	80580	11320	2600	19880
Dividends Paid	-17500	-34443	-47324	-49158	-52062	-53107	-53336	-57005	-25378	-64327
	710570	36462	-43139	-48938	-43502	-49177	27244	-45685	-22778	-44447
Lenders										
Issue/Repayment of Loans	280015	19865	-20	-136	-160	-5020	5128	-301	-3566	-1200
Interest	-14742	-17122	-17557	-18943	-15264	-16558	-14862	-15639	-16486	-15926
	265273	2743	-17577	-19079	-15424	-21578	-9734	-15940	-20052	-17126
Externally generated funds	975843	39205	-60716	-68017	-58926	-70755	17510	-61625	-42830	-61573

JOHN BROWN AND COMPANY LTD
FUNDING 1881-1914

Financing for year to 31 March	1891	1892	1893	1894	1895	1896	1897	1898	1899	1900
Internal Finance										
Operating Profit before interest and depreciation invested in	226145	203031	111623	19068	125441	225107	196641	88357	174667	377010
Stock	-8620	40679	-71952	17609	47607	-48620	-13197	11956	20533	490428
Debtors	49943	14292	-41550	-64536	49080	-14007	2673	-38775	49957	397423
Creditors	18589	82582	4377	-70717	-43132	121519	13024	-47594	-70603	-460305
Change in Working Capital	59912	137553	-109125	-117644	53555	58892	2500	-74413	-113	427546
Cash Flow from operations	166233	65478	220748	136712	71886	166215	194141	162770	174780	-50536
invested in										
Cash & Bank	7989	-5368	6793	-1870	-1603	1869	-1153	2322	228	-1100
Fixed Assets	68376	115319	68104	106236	102431	87459	60847	55814	100043	882796
Free Cash	89868	-44473	145851	32346	-28942	76887	134447	104634	74509	-932232
External Finance										
Shareholders										
Issue of Ordinary Share Capital	0	119955	45	-250	90000	0	0	0	0	1026000
Dividends Paid	-71415	-84111	-90946	-67000	-53153	-56998	-78750	-78750	-71500	-107750
	-71415	35844	-90901	-67250	36847	-56998	-78750	-78750	-71500	918250
Lenders										
Issue/Repayment of Loans	-2810	25255	-41735	48510	5650	-7150	-43680	-15600	7100	50133
Interest	-15643	-16626	-13215	-13606	-13555	-12739	-12017	-10284	-10109	-36151
	-18453	8629	-54950	34904	-7905	-19889	-55697	-25884	-3009	13982
Externally generated funds	-89868	44473	-145851	-32346	28942	-76887	-134447	-104634	-74509	932232

JOHN BROWN AND COMPANY LTD
FUNDING 1881-1914

Financing for year to 31 March	1901	1902	1903	1904	1905	1906	1907	1908	1909	1910
Internal Finance										
Operating Profit before interest and depreciation	**511251**	**310624**	**258656**	**231845**	**279994**	**295111**	**311655**	**324625**	**299080**	**298314**
invested in										
Stock	-205853	-159927	217009	-88827	-167923	148061	433	-139952	92791	136045
Debtors	-64888	-123792	-162755	108570	422110	-351069	89786	44710	30148	-66635
Creditors	465478	104263	-107834	89659	-208509	50062	-152661	-115716	-57521	-15956
Change in Working Capital	**194737**	**-179456**	**-53580**	**109402**	**45678**	**-152946**	**-62442**	**-210958**	**65418**	**53454**
Cash Flow from operations	**316514**	**490080**	**312236**	**122443**	**234316**	**448057**	**374097**	**535583**	**233662**	**244860**
invested in										
Cash & Bank	2500	1709	-636	405	1268	-3008	-585	289	2238	1197
Fixed Assets	98867	159932	443757	33158	98403	476147	206601	1406132	70189	395834
Free Cash	**215147**	**328439**	**-130885**	**88880**	**134645**	**-25082**	**168081**	**-870838**	**161235**	**-152171**
External Finance										
Shareholders										
Issue of Ordinary Share Capital	0	0	330000	0	0	0	0	1006157	135	300500
Dividends Paid	-199356	-299000	-235000	-183000	-146500	-158666	-183000	-191750	-228512	-197512
	-199356	**-299000**	**95000**	**-183000**	**-146500**	**-158666**	**-183000**	**814407**	**-228377**	**102988**
Lenders										
Issue/Repayment of Loans	-3560	-18000	48500	110250	31475	205190	42825	89970	101185	86655
Interest	-12231	-11439	-12615	-16130	-19620	-21442	-27906	-33539	-34043	-37472
	-15791	**-29439**	**35885**	**94120**	**11855**	**183748**	**14919**	**56431**	**67142**	**49183**
Externally generated funds	**-215147**	**-328439**	**130885**	**-88880**	**-134645**	**25082**	**-168081**	**870838**	**-161235**	**152171**

JOHN BROWN AND COMPANY LTD
FUNDING 1881-1914

Financing for year to 31 March	1911	1912	1913	1914
Internal Finance				
Operating Profit before interest and depreciation	**314756**	**344367**	**394593**	**508505**
invested in				
Stock	89568	-46490	334256	-100343
Debtors	14794	-6252	286211	-88621
Creditors	-74534	-8308	-494196	404273
Change in Working Capital	**29828**	**-61050**	**126271**	**215309**
Cash Flow from operations	**284928**	**405417**	**268322**	**293196**
invested in				
Cash & Bank	-2465	5404	-3922	19
Fixed Assets	402534	249373	248449	143615
Free Cash	**-115141**	**150640**	**23795**	**149562**
External Finance				
Shareholders				
Issue of Ordinary Share Capital	204500	0	150000	0
Dividends Paid	-206501	-214395	-216725	-223031
	-2001	**-214395**	**-66725**	**-223031**
Lenders				
Issue/Repayment of Loans	161440	113395	98688	133805
Interest	-44298	-49640	-55758	-60336
	117142	**63755**	**42930**	**73469**
Externally generated funds	**115141**	**-150640**	**-23795**	**-149562**

JOHN BROWN AND COMPANY LTD
FUNDING 1881-1914

Financing for year to 31 March	Summary 1882-1889	percentage 1882-1889	Summary 1890-1914	percentage 1890-1914	Summary 1882-1914	percentage 1882-1914
Internal Finance						
Operating Profit before interest and depreciation	**565724**	**184.78**	**6562364**	**-4121.44**	**7128088**	**4851.38**
invested in						
Stock	-3270	-1.07	678956	-426.41	675686	459.87
Debtors	26454	8.64	551458	-346.34	577912	393.33
Creditors	-36930	-12.06	-614727	386.07	-651657	-443.52
Change in Working Capital	**-13746**	**-4.49**	**615687**	**-366.68**	**601941**	**409.68**
Cash Flow from operations	**579470**	**189.27**	**5946677**	**-3734.76**	**6526147**	**4441.70**
invested in						
Cash & Bank	4540	1.48	2041	-1.28	6581	4.48
Fixed Assets	268776	87.79	6103861	-3833.48	6372637	4337.22
Free Cash	**306154**	**100.00**	**-159225**	**100.00**	**146929**	**100.00**
External Finance						
Shareholders						
Issue of Ordinary Share Capital	182300	59.55	3246922	-2039.20	3429222	2333.93
Dividends Paid	-371813	-121.45	-3707648	2328.56	-4079461	-2776.48
	-189513	**-61.90**	**-460726**	**289.36**	**-650239**	**-442.55**
Lenders						
Issue/Repayment of Loans	15790	5.16	1226291	-770.16	1242081	845.36
Interest	-132431	-43.26	-606340	380.81	-738771	-502.81
	-116641	**-38.10**	**619951**	**-389.36**	**503310**	**342.55**
Externally generated funds	**-306154**	**-100.00**	**159225**	**-100.00**	**-146929**	**-100.00**

NORTH'S NAVIGATION (1889) COLLIERIES LTD
FUNDING 1889-1914

Financing for year to 28 December	Incorporated 1889 1889	1890	1891	1892	missing 1893	2 years 1894	1895	1896	1897	1898
Internal Finance										
Operating Profit before interest and depreciation	**73559**	**52519**	**40840**	**23408**	**0**	**46531**	**-1165**	**7077**	**27315**	**22667**
invested in										
Stock	16398	16132	-5406	-298		8119	-14850	-4295	-4113	2328
Debtors	37176	21838	5323	-2586		-13274	-11756	5804	9978	7986
Creditors	-20874	-25091	-12123	4785		255	13042	-19542	-4807	-7438
Change in Working Capital	**32700**	**12879**	**-12206**	**1901**	**0**	**-4900**	**-13564**	**-18033**	**1058**	**2876**
Cash Flow from operations	**40859**	**39640**	**53046**	**21507**	**0**	**51431**	**12399**	**25110**	**26257**	**19791**
invested in										
Cash & Bank	61470	-54363	302	5034		17007	-13507	8382	-4790	-16948
Fixed Assets	359395	54031	61660	32345		24541	6903	14224	18551	15900
Free Cash	**-380006**	**39972**	**-8916**	**-15872**	**0**	**9883**	**19003**	**2504**	**12496**	**20839**
External Finance										
Shareholders										
Issue of Ordinary Share Capital	400000	0	49166	834		0	0	0	0	0
Dividends Paid	-19994	-39972	-40250	-24282		-35563	-16503	-4	-9996	-14934
	380006	**-39972**	**8916**	**-23448**	**0**	**-35563**	**-16503**	**-4**	**-9996**	**-14934**
Lenders										
Issue/Repayment of Loans	0	0	0	39320		25680	-2500	-2500	-2500	-2500
Interest										-3405
	0	**0**	**0**	**39320**	**0**	**25680**	**-2500**	**-2500**	**-2500**	**-5905**
Externally generated funds	**380006**	**-39972**	**8916**	**15872**	**0**	**-9883**	**-19003**	**-2504**	**-12496**	**-20839**

NORTH'S NAVIGATION (1889) COLLIERIES LTD
FUNDING 1889-1914

Financing for year to 28 December	1899	1900	1901	1902	1903	1904	1905	1906	1907	1908
Internal Finance										
Operating Profit before interest and depreciation	**91753**	**228123**	**144341**	**102415**	**71474**	**70025**	**74999**	**80956**	**142854**	**66756**
invested in										
Stock	1896	3632	-2874	1813	-2289	2855	-5185	4818	-1825	3913
Debtors	6083	18869	16821	-23338	-1669	-6626	5810	4698	-8512	-1910
Creditors	-2857	-11006	-33031	-2714	8522	11001	15495	8430	-2683	-3334
Change in Working Capital	**5122**	**11495**	**-19084**	**-24239**	**4564**	**7230**	**16120**	**17946**	**-13020**	**-1331**
Cash Flow from operations	**86631**	**216628**	**163425**	**126654**	**66910**	**62795**	**58879**	**63010**	**155874**	**68087**
invested in										
Cash & Bank	27996	35563	-4852	436	-32548	-4991	1908	-12941	175133	-89647
Fixed Assets	15134	60558	40102	58217	23426	2769	3945	11013	-84354	62802
Free Cash	**43501**	**120507**	**128175**	**68001**	**76032**	**65017**	**53026**	**64938**	**65095**	**94932**
External Finance										
Shareholders										
Issue of Ordinary Share Capital	0	0	0	0	0	0	0	0	0	0
Dividends Paid	-37477	-65003	-124996	-64901	-74910	-65017	-53026	-64938	-65095	-94932
	-37477	**-65003**	**-124996**	**-64901**	**-74910**	**-65017**	**-53026**	**-64938**	**-65095**	**-94932**
Lenders										
Issue/Repayment of Loans	-2600	-52400	0	0	0	0	0	0	0	0
Interest	-3424	-3104	-3179	-3100	-1122	0	0	0	0	0
	-6024	**-55504**	**-3179**	**-3100**	**-1122**	**0**	**0**	**0**	**0**	**0**
Externally generated funds	**-43501**	**-120507**	**-128175**	**-68001**	**-76032**	**-65017**	**-53026**	**-64938**	**-65095**	**-94932**

NORTH'S NAVIGATION (1889) COLLIERIES LTD
FUNDING 1889-1914

Financing for year to 28 December	1909	1910	1911	1912	1913	1914
Internal Finance						
Operating Profit before interest and depreciation	**52249**	**54188**	**62262**	**71642**	**111144**	**81578**
invested in						
Stock	-191	-3440	9272	-521	-4571	5400
Debtors	-7190	11981	3325	8662	-1584	-1767
Creditors	9284	-10219	-30082	-573	2099	-1606
Change in Working Capital	**1903**	**-1678**	**-17485**	**7568**	**-4056**	**2027**
Cash Flow from operations	**50346**	**55866**	**79747**	**64074**	**115200**	**79551**
invested in						
Cash & Bank	-14175	-33589	-22502	-12188	28277	-10754
Fixed Assets	23644	40385	47322	23300	33836	20305
Free Cash	**40877**	**49070**	**54927**	**52962**	**53087**	**70000**
External Finance						
Shareholders						
Issue of Ordinary Share Capital	0	0	0	0	0	0
Dividends Paid	-40877	-49070	-54927	-52962	-53087	-70000
	-40877	**-49070**	**-54927**	**-52962**	**-53087**	**-70000**
Lenders						
Issue/Repayment of Loans	0	0	0	0	0	0
Interest	0	0	0	0	0	0
	0	**0**	**0**	**0**	**0**	**0**
Externally generated funds	**-40877**	**-49070**	**-54927**	**-52962**	**-53087**	**-70000**

NORTH'S NAVIGATION (1889) COLLIERIES LTD
FUNDING 1889-1914

Financing for year to 28 December	Summary 1889	percentage 1889	Summary 1890-1914	percentage 1890-1914	Summary 1889-1914	percentage 1889-1914
Internal Finance						
Operating Profit before interest and depreciation	**73559**	**-19.36**	**1725951**	**146.26**	**1799510**	**224.92**
invested in						
Stock	16398	-4.32	10320	0.87	26718	3.34
Debtors	37176	-9.78	46966	3.98	84142	10.52
Creditors	-20874	5.49	-94193	-7.98	-115067	-14.38
Change in Working Capital	**32700**	**-8.61**	**-36907**	**-3.13**	**-4207**	**-0.53**
Cash Flow from operations	**40859**	**-10.75**	**1762858**	**149.39**	**1803717**	**225.45**
invested in						
Cash & Bank	61470	-16.18	-27757	-2.35	33713	4.21
Fixed Assets	359395	-94.58	610559	51.74	969954	121.24
Free Cash	**-380006**	**100.00**	**1180056**	**100.00**	**800050**	**100.00**
External Finance						
Shareholders						
Issue of Ordinary Share Capital	400000	-105.26	50000	4.24	450000	56.25
Dividends Paid	-19994	5.26	-1212722	-102.77	-1232716	-154.08
	380006	**-100.00**	**-1162722**	**-98.53**	**-782716**	**-97.83**
Lenders						
Issue/Repayment of Loans	0	0.00	0	0.00	0	0.00
Interest	0	0.00	-17334	-1.47	-17334	-2.17
	0	**0.00**	**-17334**	**-1.47**	**-17334**	**-2.17**
Externally generated funds	**380006**	**-100.00**	**-1180056**	**-100.00**	**-800050**	**-100.00**

PEARSON KNOWLES COAL AND IRON COMPANY LTD
FUNDING 1874-1914

Financing for year to 30 June	1874	1875	1876	1877	1878	1879	1880	1881	1882	1883	1884
	Incorporated 1873 and 1899										
Internal Finance											
Operating Profit before interest and depreciation invested in	**41845**	**52754**	**56121**	**7021**	**10825**	**10132**	**59687**	**43469**	**52560**	**46396**	**46118**
Stock	87964	6642	-613	-17111	19496	40424	37826	-31499	20868	9565	2055
Debtors	87737	-21157	260	-2246	-6928	3551	1438	15963	1178	-1056	-4643
Creditors	-80681	39486	-11905	1828	-5102	3013	-3373	-16324	-5786	-1895	-724
Change in Working Capital	**95020**	**24971**	**-12258**	**-17529**	**7466**	**46988**	**35891**	**-31860**	**16260**	**6614**	**-3312**
Cash Flow from operations invested in	**-53175**	**27783**	**68379**	**24550**	**3359**	**-36856**	**23796**	**75329**	**36300**	**39782**	**49430**
Cash & Bank	33641	-10394	6848	-7811	-1940	11534	-21182	15971	-10759	296	2108
Fixed Assets	733184	11332	11731	7461	5299	-48390	18854	8334	12567	4194	6742
Free Cash	**-820000**	**26845**	**49800**	**24900**	**0**	**0**	**26124**	**51024**	**34492**	**35292**	**40580**
External Finance											
Shareholders											
Issue of Ordinary Share Capital	820000	10000	0	0	0	0	0	0	0	-800	0
Dividends Paid	0	-36845	-49800	-24900	0	0	-26124	-51024	-34492	-34492	-40580
	820000	-26845	-49800	-24900	0	0	-26124	-51024	-34492	-35292	-40580
Lenders											
Issue/Repayment of Loans Interest	0	0	0	0	0	0	0	0	0	0	0
(estimated at 4% post 1906 only)	0	0	0	0	0	0	0	0	0	0	0
Externally generated funds	**820000**	**-26845**	**-49800**	**-24900**	**0**	**0**	**-26124**	**-51024**	**-34492**	**-35292**	**-40580**

PEARSON KNOWLES COAL AND IRON COMPANY LTD
FUNDING 1874-1914

Financing for year to 30 June	1885	1886	1887	1888	1889	1890	1891	1892	1893	1894	1895
Internal Finance											
Operating Profit before interest and depreciation	**36440**	**18266**	**25566**	**24858**	**49463**	**115687**	**68997**	**52097**	**30130**	**23486**	**23607**
invested in											
Stock	857	-16543	-3204	1498	12267	17647	-7433	16361	-6992	-16689	47868
Debtors	489	8782	3342	-7231	5543	36420	3368	-13668	-8102	-7807	-11043
Creditors	7225	-3330	-6710	-341	11230	7870	-2304	-7435	-335	9527	-3112
Change in Working Capital	**8571**	**-11091**	**-6572**	**-6074**	**29040**	**61937**	**-6369**	**-4742**	**-15429**	**-14969**	**33713**
Cash Flow from operations	**27869**	**29357**	**32138**	**30932**	**20423**	**53750**	**75366**	**56839**	**45559**	**38455**	**-10106**
invested in											
Cash & Bank	1014	-9471	9025	7371	2487	-3048	4754	-19304	-6064	9862	6064
Fixed Assets	1563	10479	3936	4384	-7356	13707	19122	33597	32925	22239	-22497
Free Cash	**25292**	**28349**	**19177**	**19177**	**25292**	**43091**	**51490**	**42546**	**18698**	**6354**	**6327**
External Finance											
Shareholders											
Issue of Ordinary Share Capital	0	0	0	0	0	0	0	0	0	0	0
Dividends Paid	-25292	-28349	-19177	-19177	-25292	-43091	-51490	-42546	-18698	-6354	-6327
	-25292	-28349	-19177	-19177	-25292	-43091	-51490	-42546	-18698	-6354	-6327
Lenders											
Issue/Repayment of Loans	0	0	0	0	0	0	0	0	0	0	0
Interest											
(estimated at 4% post 1906 only)	0	0	0	0	0	0	0	0	0	0	0
Externally generated funds	**-25292**	**-28349**	**-19177**	**-19177**	**-25292**	**-43091**	**-51490**	**-42546**	**-18698**	**-6354**	**-6327**

PEARSON KNOWLES COAL AND IRON COMPANY LTD
FUNDING 1874-1914

Financing for year to 30 June	1896	1897	1898	1899	1900	1901	1902	1903	1904	1905	1906
Internal Finance											
Operating Profit before interest and depreciation invested in	**23321**	**43215**	**37453**	**75042**	**138644**	**142425**	**62865**	**53426**	**46748**	**57187**	**62866**
Stock	15274	16017	-15190	-3760	14301	-2439	-11845	-7718	409	-94	36918
Debtors	5939	-5991	21098	18384	19157	-31132	-2374	4994	-5215	5488	3401
Creditors	-11586	6624	-25236	-13517	25693	32095	10988	-16319	11683	831	-19694
Change in Working Capital	**9627**	**16650**	**-19328**	**1107**	**59151**	**-1476**	**-3231**	**-19043**	**6877**	**6225**	**20625**
Cash Flow from operations invested in	**13694**	**26565**	**56781**	**73935**	**79493**	**143901**	**66096**	**72469**	**39871**	**50962**	**42241**
Cash & Bank	-12069	-8933	3015	21284	38929	17158	-16077	24691	-6654	8095	-15394
Fixed Assets	13137	15558	22523	31180	11130	39523	3997	6251	10925	7252	15935
Free Cash	**12626**	**19940**	**31243**	**21471**	**29434**	**87220**	**78176**	**41527**	**35600**	**35615**	**41700**
External Finance											
Shareholders											
Issue of Ordinary Share Capital	0	-1000	-500	0	32300	0	0	0	0	0	0
Dividends Paid	-12626	-18940	-30743	-21471	-61734	-87220	-78176	-41527	-35600	-35615	-41700
	-12626	-19940	-31243	-21471	-29434	-87220	-78176	-41527	-35600	-35615	-41700
Lenders											
Issue/Repayment of Loans	0	0	0	0	0	0	0	0	0	0	0
Interest (estimated at 4% post 1906 only)	0	0	0	0	0	0	0	0	0	0	0
Externally generated funds	**-12626**	**-19940**	**-31243**	**-21471**	**-29434**	**-87220**	**-78176**	**-41527**	**-35600**	**-35615**	**-41700**

PEARSON KNOWLES COAL AND IRON COMPANY LTD
FUNDING 1874-1914

Financing for year to 30 June	1907	1908	1909	1910	1911	1912	1913	1914
					Consolidated Accounts from 1911			
Internal Finance								
Operating Profit before interest and depreciation	**115023**	**120353**	**65523**	**59855**	**77634**	**77304**	**125606**	**107285**
invested in								
Stock	-12166	-21592	-10369	26267	6531	24537	-9636	-35462
Debtors	52207	-35315	33588	31076	3082	16420	10720	-16000
Creditors	-12521	28189	3501	-22386	13738	-34144	-12576	40665
Change in Working Capital	**27520**	**-28718**	**26720**	**34957**	**23351**	**6813**	**-11492**	**-10797**
Cash Flow from operations	**87503**	**149071**	**38803**	**24898**	**54283**	**70491**	**137098**	**118082**
invested in								
Cash & Bank	18698	57089	-79038	35890	68710	11204	-132508	82894
Fixed Assets	125237	4764	11981	17946	50455	41421	207998	61831
Free Cash	**-56432**	**87218**	**105860**	**-28938**	**-64882**	**17866**	**61608**	**-26643**
External Finance								
Shareholders								
Issue of Ordinary Share Capital	0	0	0	0	105768	34232	0	0
Dividends Paid	-47800	-82875	-66405	-38646	-34230	-43042	-59372	-65117
	-47800	-82875	-66405	-38646	71538	-8810	-59372	-65117
Lenders								
Issue/Repayment of Loans	108575	0	-36575	73400	0	-2500	4500	102600
Interest	-4343	-4343	-2880	-5816	-6656	-6556	-6736	-10840
(estimated at 4% post 1906 only)	104232	-4343	-39455	67584	-6656	-9056	-2236	91760
Externally generated funds	**56432**	**-87218**	**-105860**	**28938**	**64882**	**-17866**	**-61608**	**26643**

PEARSON KNOWLES COAL AND IRON COMPANY LTD
FUNDING 1874-1914

Financing for year to 30 June	Summary 1874-1889	percentage 1874-1889	Summary 1890-1914	percentage 1890-1914	Summary 1874-1914	percentage 1874-1914
Internal Finance						
Operating Profit before interest and depreciation	**581521**	**140.58**	**1805779**	**258.44**	**2387300**	**837.48**
invested in						
Stock	170492	41.22	60745	8.69	231237	81.12
Debtors	85022	20.55	128695	18.42	213717	74.97
Creditors	-73389	-17.74	10239	1.47	-63150	-22.15
Change in Working Capital	**182125**	**44.03**	**199679**	**28.58**	**381804**	**133.94**
Cash Flow from operations	**399396**	**96.55**	**1606100**	**229.86**	**2005496**	**703.54**
invested in						
Cash & Bank	28738	6.95	109248	15.64	137986	48.41
Fixed Assets	784314	189.61	798137	114.23	1582451	555.13
Free Cash	**-413656**	**-100.00**	**698715**	**100.00**	**285059**	**100.00**
External Finance						
Shareholders						
Issue of Ordinary Share Capital	829200	200.46	170800	24.44	1000000	350.80
Dividends Paid	-415544	-100.46	-1071345	-153.33	-1486889	-521.61
	413656	100.00	-900545	-128.89	-486889	-170.80
Lenders						
Issue/Repayment of Loans	0	0.00	250000	35.78	250000	87.70
Interest	0	0.00	-48170	-6.89	-48170	-16.90
(estimated at 4% post 1906 only)	0	0.00	201830	28.89	201830	70.80
Externally generated funds	**413656**	**100.00**	**-698715**	**-100.00**	**-285059**	**-100.00**

POWELL DUFFRYN STEAM COAL COMPANY LTD
FUNDING 1888-1914

Incorporated 1864   From 1888 to 1899 Debtors included Cash and Bills Receivable

Financing for year to 31 December	1888 cumulative figures to 1888	1889	1890	1891	1892	1893	1894	1895	1896	1897
Internal Finance	*balancing figure*									
Operating Profit before interest and depreciation	27094	79471	135650	118427	50217	25086	72786	40368	56528	66728
invested in										
Stock	114303	-6790	2963	11656	4006	-14394	7295	-2926	500	-5617
Debtors	99660	50326	36154	-3549	-37391	67374	-55127	-29348	81172	20126
Creditors	-92236	4234	-25896	-21108	-19676	29252	9637	-468	-29754	37379
Change in Working Capital	121727	47770	13221	-13001	-53061	82232	-38195	-32742	51918	51888
Cash Flow from operations	-94633	31701	122429	131428	103278	-57146	110981	73110	4610	14840
invested in										
Cash & Bank (with Debts to 1899)	0	0	0	0	0	0	0	0	0	0
Fixed Assets	810869	13729	21864	24670	27059	9049	61439	7959	-5784	23582
Free Cash	-905502	-17972	100565	106758	76219	-66195	49542	65151	10394	-8742
External Finance										
Shareholders										
Issue of Ordinary Share Capital	751100	0	0	0	0	0	0	0	0	0
Dividends Paid	0	-2955	-66464	-92939	-61876	-24601	-24601	-46345	-24601	-24601
	751100	**-2955**	**-66464**	**-92939**	**-61876**	**-24601**	**-24601**	**-46345**	**-24601**	**-24601**
Lenders										
Issue/Repayment of Loans	154402	-6651	-27015	-7396	-7800	98722	-13673	-7489	25063	45671
Interest		-8366	-7086	-6423	-6543	-7926	-11268	-11317	-10856	-12328
(estimated at 4% post 1907)	**154402**	**-15017**	**-34101**	**-13819**	**-14343**	**90796**	**-24941**	**-18806**	**14207**	**33343**
Externally generated funds	**905502**	**-17972**	**-100565**	**-106758**	**-76219**	**66195**	**-49542**	**-65151**	**-10394**	**8742**

POWELL DUFFRYN STEAM COAL COMPANY LTD
FUNDING 1888-1914

Financing for year to 31 December	1898	1899	1900	1901	1902	1903	1904	1905	1906	1907
Internal Finance										
Operating Profit before interest and depreciation	30238	125423	337032	220730	179538	149622	212560	150360	204195	424788
invested in										
Stock	28393	-32226	45809	-9331	37906	20355	51637	-4591	15171	24884
Debtors	-79581	126553	-95594	-10119	27033	68853	-77622	29834	693	54560
Creditors	-17824	21768	-11535	-15772	-39865	-18372	16158	-6288	-25586	-9861
Change in Working Capital	**-69012**	**116095**	**-61320**	**-35222**	**25074**	**70836**	**-9827**	**18955**	**-9722**	**69583**
Cash Flow from operations	**99250**	**9328**	**398352**	**255952**	**154464**	**78786**	**222387**	**131405**	**213917**	**355205**
invested in										
Cash & Bank (with Debts to 1899)	0	0	109827	23415	-9192	-52988	-5879	38678	8265	252875
Fixed Assets	58354	14353	209124	170247	96986	65981	157473	66669	139431	198931
Free Cash	**40896**	**-5025**	**79401**	**62290**	**66670**	**65793**	**70793**	**26058**	**66221**	**-96601**
External Finance										
Shareholders										
Issue of Ordinary Share Capital	0	27595	0	3240	-1140	0	0	0	0	198180
Dividends Paid	-30814	-19558	-54314	-52835	-52835	-53098	-58098	-53098	-53097	-53097
	-30814	**8037**	**-54314**	**-49595**	**-53975**	**-53098**	**-58098**	**-53098**	**-53097**	**145083**
Lenders										
Issue/Repayment of Loans	3674	8784	-12392	0	0	0	0	39735	-429	-37759
Interest (estimated at 4% post 1907)	-13756	-11796	-12695	-12695	-12695	-12695	-12695	-12695	-12695	-10723
	-10082	**-3012**	**-25087**	**-12695**	**-12695**	**-12695**	**-12695**	**27040**	**-13124**	**-48482**
Externally generated funds	**-40896**	**5025**	**-79401**	**-62290**	**-66670**	**-65793**	**-70793**	**-26058**	**-66221**	**96601**

POWELL DUFFRYN STEAM COAL COMPANY LTD
FUNDING 1888-1914

Financing for year to 31 December	1908	1909	1910	1911	1912	1913	1914
Internal Finance							
Operating Profit before interest and depreciation	383014	231871	304884	250660	283416	399307	447764
invested in							
Stock	50279	-1023	2601	45094	6647	47280	-47368
Debtors	5856	-24626	-32157	61194	68854	-32760	-10787
Creditors	-7260	4516	71542	-76718	9474	-75610	-6488
Change in Working Capital	**48875**	**-21133**	**41986**	**29570**	**84975**	**-61090**	**-64643**
Cash Flow from operations	**334139**	**253004**	**262898**	**221090**	**198441**	**460397**	**512407**
invested in							
Cash & Bank (with Debts to 1899)	-232554	-73984	77017	-51214	45843	65821	17939
Fixed Assets	211926	147946	99452	163513	93254	177706	158138
Free Cash	**354767**	**179042**	**86429**	**108791**	**59344**	**216870**	**336330**
External Finance							
Shareholders							
Issue of Ordinary Share Capital	1820	0	51556	77348	126423	53729	173
Dividends Paid	-175598	-174348	-133243	-181352	-196294	-265075	-338606
	-173778	**-174348**	**-81687**	**-104004**	**-69871**	**-211346**	**-338433**
Lenders							
Issue/Repayment of Loans	-177807	-1575	-1691	-1808	14069	-2065	5794
Interest	-3182	-3119	-3051	-2979	-3542	-3459	-3691
(estimated at 4% post 1907)	**-180989**	**-4694**	**-4742**	**-4787**	**10527**	**-5524**	**2103**
Externally generated funds	**-354767**	**-179042**	**-86429**	**-108791**	**-59344**	**-216870**	**-336330**

POWELL DUFFRYN STEAM COAL COMPANY LTD
FUNDING 1888-1914

Financing for year to 31 December	Summary 1888-1889	percentage 1888-1889	Summary 1890-1914	percentage 1890-1914	Summary 1888-1914	percentage 1888-1914
Internal Finance						
Operating Profit before interest and depreciation invested in	**106565**	*12.01*	**4901193**	*238.88*	**5007758**	*430.13*
Stock	107513	12.11	285000	13.89	392513	33.71
Debtors	149986	16.90	159595	7.78	309581	26.59
Creditors	-88002	-9.92	-208355	-10.15	-296357	-25.46
Change in Working Capital	**169497**	*19.10*	**236240**	*11.51*	**405737**	*34.85*
Cash Flow from operations invested in	**-62932**	*-7.09*	**4664953**	*227.36*	**4602021**	*395.28*
Cash & Bank (with Debts to 1899)	0	0.00	213869	10.42	213869	18.37
Fixed Assets	824598	92.91	2399322	116.94	3223920	276.91
Free Cash	**-887530**	*-100.00*	**2051762**	*100.00*	**1164232**	*100.00*
External Finance						
Shareholders						
Issue of Ordinary Share Capital	751100	84.63	538924	26.27	1290024	110.80
Dividends Paid	-2955	-0.33	-2311388	-112.65	-2314343	-198.79
	748145	*84.30*	**-1772464**	*-86.39*	**-1024319**	*-87.98*
Lenders						
Issue/Repayment of Loans	147751	16.65	-57387	-2.80	90364	7.76
Interest (estimated at 4% post 1907)	-8366	-0.94	-221911	-10.82	-230277	-19.78
	139385	*15.70*	**-279298**	*-13.61*	**-139913**	*-12.02*
Externally generated funds	**887530**	*100.00*	**-2051762**	*-100.00*	**-1164232**	*-100.00*

THE RHYMNEY IRON COMPANY LTD
FUNDING 1882-1914

Financing for year to 31 March	1881	1882	1883	1884	1885	1886	1887	1888	1889	1890	1891	1892
	Incorporated 1871 cumulative figures to 1881											
Internal Finance	*balancing figure*											
Operating Profit before interest and depreciation	94074	26501	23032	24761	-1574	34243	-29909	21065	-16725	42640	53386	22534
invested in												
Stock	314225	-37859	98	4510	-47981	-38262	-62070	7702	-4715	48	715	-43565
Debtors	66420	10942	-554	-421	7632	-2455	-6263	7410	7618	-5702	6987	3530
Creditors	-251362	32752	59998	16289	28001	30146	1893	-11051	3292	-5487	7436	1703
Change in Working Capital	**129283**	**5835**	**59542**	**20378**	**-12348**	**-10571**	**-66440**	**4061**	**6195**	**-11141**	**15138**	**-38332**
Cash Flow from operations	**-35209**	**20666**	**-36510**	**4383**	**10774**	**44814**	**36531**	**17004**	**-22920**	**53781**	**38248**	**60866**
invested in												
Cash & Bank	27039	9799	-26191	-105	2454	3676	1838	-4651	6148	8752	-12552	-4752
Fixed Assets	790170	41258	41108	19174	4180	0	5358	14476	12950	15120	21458	29608
Free Cash	**-852418**	**-30391**	**-51427**	**-14686**	**4140**	**41138**	**29335**	**7179**	**-42018**	**29909**	**29342**	**36010**
External Finance												
Shareholders												
Issue of Ordinary Share Capital	639734	74726	0	49447	795	175	250	0	0	670	20	0
Dividends Paid	-9535	-6347	-1	-7720	0	0	4706	289	303	-14195	-30889	-22385
	630199	**68379**	**-1**	**41727**	**795**	**175**	**4956**	**289**	**303**	**-13525**	**-30869**	**-22385**
Lenders												
Issue/Repayment of Loans	236000	-22570	66353	-12463	11890	-20660	-17350	8793	58107	2000	17800	3060
Interest	-13781	-15418	-14925	-14578	-16825	-20653	-16941	-16261	-16392	-18384	-16273	-16685
	222219	**-37988**	**51428**	**-27041**	**-4935**	**-41313**	**-34291**	**-7468**	**41715**	**-16384**	**1527**	**-13625**
Externally generated funds	**852418**	**30391**	**51427**	**14686**	**-4140**	**-41138**	**-29335**	**-7179**	**42018**	**-29909**	**-29342**	**-36010**

THE RHYMNEY IRON COMPANY LTD
FUNDING 1882-1914

Financing for year to 31 March	1893	1894	1895	1896	1897	1898	1899	1900	1901	1902	1903	1904
Internal Finance												
Operating Profit before interest and depreciation	22943	75422	47189	28197	18301	38244	26396	111497	159265	103868	65734	40993
invested in												
Stock	-22343	-9445	-5726	-2532	-1834	-3050	523	-6406	89	-3557	1335	-641
Debtors	1427	9193	14972	568	2016	10434	-9075	26645	6820	-8987	-30909	71903
Creditors	3026	-14194	-15529	66747	-2352	14524	5314	-7866	-3994	5487	-10221	-14739
Change in Working Capital	**-17890**	**-14446**	**-6283**	**64783**	**-2170**	**21908**	**-3238**	**12373**	**2915**	**-7057**	**-39795**	**56523**
Cash Flow from operations	**40833**	**89868**	**53472**	**-36586**	**20471**	**16336**	**29634**	**99124**	**156350**	**110925**	**105529**	**-15530**
invested in												
Cash & Bank	-44	58892	801	-59652	2103	21007	-16394	60685	-20178	-26506	-25880	1000
Fixed Assets	25594	18225	0	-7839	-8106	13080	16043	2591	79089	41272	75320	-62521
Free Cash	**15283**	**12751**	**52671**	**30905**	**26474**	**-17751**	**29985**	**35848**	**97439**	**96159**	**56089**	**45991**
External Finance												
Shareholders												
Issue of Ordinary Share Capital	0	0	0	0	0	35614	15165	749	0	0	0	0
Dividends Paid	495	-13310	-35044	-13237	-8807	-196	-27641	-15147	-76189	-75109	-35239	-25341
	495	**-13310**	**-35044**	**-13237**	**-8807**	**35418**	**-12476**	**-14398**	**-76189**	**-75109**	**-35239**	**-25341**
Lenders												
Issue/Repayment of Loans	1000	18000	40	0	0	0	0	-4000	-4000	-4000	-4000	-4000
Interest	-16778	-17441	-17667	-17668	-17667	-17667	-17509	-17450	-17250	-17050	-16850	-16650
	-15778	**559**	**-17627**	**-17668**	**-17667**	**-17667**	**-17509**	**-21450**	**-21250**	**-21050**	**-20850**	**-20650**
Externally generated funds	**-15283**	**-12751**	**-52671**	**-30905**	**-26474**	**17751**	**-29985**	**-35848**	**-97439**	**-96159**	**-56089**	**-45991**

THE RHYMNEY IRON COMPANY LTD
FUNDING 1882-1914

Financing for year to 31 March	1905	1906	1907	1908	1909	1910	1911	1912	1913	1914
Internal Finance										
Operating Profit before interest and depreciation	**39091**	**41495**	**59192**	**75764**	**52047**	**51528**	**47391**	**-18470**	**70424**	**125633**
invested in										
Stock	-3084	-930	-1372	-258	5452	7440	-1658	-5896	-3978	-1713
Debtors	17441	29483	17653	11083	-11549	5702	802	-40013	41897	-17134
Creditors	-3484	14514	-14058	-7882	4406	2798	-12750	12188	-15083	-11609
Change in Working Capital	**10873**	**43067**	**2223**	**2943**	**-1691**	**15940**	**-13606**	**-33721**	**22836**	**-30456**
Cash Flow from operations	**28218**	**-1572**	**56969**	**72821**	**53738**	**35588**	**60997**	**15251**	**47588**	**156089**
invested in										
Cash & Bank	-2144	44406	-45825	-36423	-13673	1806	11822	17560	20024	25779
Fixed Assets	-10137	56064	64637	46850	60198	4593	312	5086	3177	41026
Free Cash	**40499**	**-102042**	**38157**	**62394**	**7213**	**29189**	**48863**	**-7395**	**24387**	**89284**
External Finance										
Shareholders										
Issue of Ordinary Share Capital	0	0	0	0	0	0	0	0	0	0
Dividends Paid	-20049	-18938	-18231	-44694	-18302	261	-19613	-15593	346	-64810
	-20049	**-18938**	**-18231**	**-44694**	**-18302**	**261**	**-19613**	**-15593**	**346**	**-64810**
Lenders										
Issue/Repayment of Loans	-4000	138400	3600	5650	36350	-4000	-4000	48000	0	0
Interest	-16450	-17420	-23526	-23350	-25261	-25450	-25250	-25012	-24733	-24474
	-20450	**120980**	**-19926**	**-17700**	**11089**	**-29450**	**-29250**	**22988**	**-24733**	**-24474**
Externally generated funds	**-40499**	**102042**	**-38157**	**-62394**	**-7213**	**-29189**	**-48863**	**7395**	**-24387**	**-89284**

THE RHYMNEY IRON COMPANY LTD
FUNDING 1882-1914

Financing for year to 31 March	Summary 1881-1889	percentage 1881-1889	Summary 1890-1914	percentage 1890-1914	Summary 1881-1914	percentage 1881-1914
Internal Finance						
Operating Profit before interest and depreciation invested in	175468	-19.30	1400704	173.43	1576172	-1552.97
Stock	135648	-14.92	-102386	-12.68	33262	-32.77
Debtors	90329	-9.94	155187	19.21	245516	-241.90
Creditors	-90042	9.90	-1105	-0.14	-91147	89.81
Change in Working Capital	135935	-14.95	51696	6.40	187631	-184.87
Cash Flow from operations invested in	39533	-4.35	1349008	167.03	1388541	-1368.10
Cash & Bank	20007	-2.20	10614	1.31	30621	-30.17
Fixed Assets	928674	-102.15	530740	65.71	1459414	-1437.93
Free Cash	-909148	100.00	807654	100.00	-101494	100.00
External Finance						
Shareholders						
Issue of Ordinary Share Capital	765127	-84.16	52218	6.47	817345	-805.31
Dividends Paid	-18305	2.01	-611857	-75.76	-630162	620.89
	746822	-82.15	-559639	-69.29	187183	-184.43
Lenders						
Issue/Repayment of Loans	308100	-33.89	241900	29.95	550000	-541.90
Interest	-145774	16.03	-489915	-60.66	-635689	626.33
	162326	-17.85	-248015	-30.71	-85689	84.43
Externally generated funds	909148	-100.00	-807654	-100.00	101494	-100.00

SHEEPBRIDGE COAL AND IRON COMPANY LTD
FUNDING 1865-1914

Financing for year to 25 June	Incorporated 1864 1865	1866	1867	1868	1869	1870	1871	1872	1873	1874
Internal Finance										
Operating Profit before interest and depreciation	16817	-7907	10863	16162	14148	22066	36009	48335	136484	126085
invested in										
Stock	53786	-10314	11997	8491	-42	507	-5007	-19023	17362	1022
Debtors	15406	9239	1611	-6976	12423	9587	10264	11836	16309	-20424
Creditors	-25958	-15235	-2783	17994	-7449	-21485	14132	-5844	12095	1521
Change in Working Capital	43234	-16310	10825	19509	4932	-11391	19389	-13031	45766	-17881
Cash Flow from operations	-26417	8403	38	-3347	9216	33457	16620	61366	90718	143966
invested in										
Cash & Bank	-7814	7922	635	1646	-1766	8751	-4679	3005	27203	-3904
Fixed Assets	263532	25260	14937	46911	46945	13423	15711	9455	8335	62047
Free Cash	-282135	-24779	-15534	-51904	-35963	11283	5588	48906	55180	85823
External Finance										
Shareholders										
Issue of Ordinary Share Capital	125730	43270	42445	37925	5920	23910	0	0	0	0
Dividends Paid	0	0	-6250	-5994	0	-16028	-16339	-25092	-39995	-67330
	125730	43270	36195	31931	5920	7882	-16339	-25092	-39995	-67330
Lenders										
Issue/Repayment of Loans	156405	-18491	-20661	19973	35202	-16023	12244	-23814	-15185	-18493
Interest (possibly capitalised before 1883)					-5159	-3142	-1493			
	156405	-18491	-20661	19973	30043	-19165	10751	-23814	-15185	-18493
Externally generated funds	282135	24779	15534	51904	35963	-11283	-5588	-48906	-55180	-85823

SHEEPBRIDGE COAL AND IRON COMPANY LTD
FUNDING 1865-1914

Financing for year to 25 June	1875	1876	1877	1878	1879	1880	1881	1882	1883	1884
Internal Finance										
Operating Profit before interest and depreciation invested in	62493	24788	25456	-8050	-5235	6801	12741	21321	18730	27587
Stock	1585	1471	5571	9447	-2282	-20401	1178	5007	-8404	3136
Debtors	-1673	-13905	9727	2782	5522	9730	8914	-5351	9106	-3564
Creditors	-305	-4725	-39387	15419	16725	-12637	1775	-16825	8709	-38347
Change in Working Capital	-393	-17159	-24089	27648	19965	-23308	11867	-17169	9411	-38775
Cash Flow from operations invested in	62886	41947	49545	-35698	-25200	30109	874	38490	9319	66362
Cash & Bank	-27877	849	-3821	9	158	-273	94	6	-13	-8
Fixed Assets	15502	45045	70119	33904	12990	33774	29302	35111	39852	25321
Free Cash	75261	-3947	-16753	-69611	-38348	-3392	-28522	3373	-30520	41049
External Finance										
Shareholders										
Issue of Ordinary Share Capital	0	0	0	71240	46945	3505	36396	19805	43486	8329
Dividends Paid	-60808	-44654	-18003	-8311	0	0	0	-22263	0	-5309
	-60808	-44654	-18003	62929	46945	3505	36396	-2458	43486	3020
Lenders										
Issue/Repayment of Loans	-14453	48601	34756	6682	-8597	-113	-7874	-915	-1582	-34917
Interest (possibly capitalised before 1883)									-11384	-9152
	-14453	48601	34756	6682	-8597	-113	-7874	-915	-12966	-44069
Externally generated funds	-75261	3947	16753	69611	38348	3392	28522	-3373	30520	-41049

SHEEPBRIDGE COAL AND IRON COMPANY LTD
FUNDING 1865-1914

Financing for year to 25 June	1885	1886	1887	1888	1889	1890	1891	1892	1893	1894
Internal Finance										
Operating Profit before interest and depreciation	12502	6171	12954	15868	35916	90207	79510	58460	43959	41828
invested in										
Stock	11040	-16794	-5685	-4170	3956	23235	-15652	-19265	11801	-9307
Debtors	-285	-3359	2294	2556	11712	-3349	-4504	-5826	-15293	-2177
Creditors	2700	1787	59751	-18613	-3506	-2362	6575	-3453	18200	2791
Change in Working Capital	13455	-18366	56360	-20227	12162	17524	-13581	-28544	14708	-8693
Cash Flow from operations	-953	24537	-43406	36095	23754	72683	93091	87004	29251	50521
invested in										
Cash & Bank	-44	39	-35	-12	90	10289	29570	10436	-36822	12017
Fixed Assets	24581	6634	544	-2401	14664	30587	25485	9450	-8092	-782
Free Cash	-25490	17864	-43915	38508	9000	31807	38036	67118	74165	39286
External Finance										
Shareholders										
Issue of Ordinary Share Capital	40265	817	59077	-850	2385	0	39350	15740	0	0
Dividends Paid	-5514	-5621	-5614	-5614	-5614	-30275	-49819	-52459	-31585	-35770
	34751	-4804	53463	-6464	-3229	-30275	-10469	-36719	-31585	-35770
Lenders										
Issue/Repayment of Loans	1445	-435	1	-22898	3074	6723	-19714	-25025	-39435	-1102
Interest (possibly capitalised before 1883)	-10706	-12625	-9549	-9146	-8845	-8255	-7853	-5374	-3145	-2414
	-9261	-13060	-9548	-32044	-5771	-1532	-27567	-30399	-42580	-3516
Externally generated funds	25490	-17864	43915	-38508	-9000	-31807	-38036	-67118	-74165	-39286

SHEEPBRIDGE COAL AND IRON COMPANY LTD
FUNDING 1865-1914

Financing for year to 25 June	1895	1896	1897	1898	1899	1900	1901	1902	1903	1904
Internal Finance										
Operating Profit before interest and depreciation invested in	27536	18517	41114	55293	84876	211547	249111	98467	87138	80380
Stock	5798	-11711	5565	543	-731	11182	-2020	-276	16418	9039
Debtors	3599	4325	8230	-3468	2154	11599	-1271	-8359	-787	-14999
Creditors	-2769	-8238	1224	-9282	7057	-881	-18617	-9614	-6934	-4305
Change in Working Capital	6628	-15624	15019	-12207	8480	21900	-21908	-18249	8697	-10265
Cash Flow from operations	20908	34141	26095	67500	76396	189647	271019	116716	78441	90645
invested in										
Cash & Bank	-11867	8540	-12993	19885	-8892	24665	-16641	11720	-13843	5270
Fixed Assets	-290	6446	15067	13498	47633	99767	111981	22154	19601	15660
Free Cash	33065	19155	24021	34117	37655	65215	175679	82842	72683	69715
External Finance										
Shareholders										
Issue of Ordinary Share Capital	0	0	0	0	1675	0	0	0	0	0
Dividends Paid	-28919	-15218	-22069	-33030	-38510	-62743	-170303	-80670	-71707	-68719
	-28919	-15218	-22069	-33030	-36835	-62743	-170303	-80670	-71707	-68719
Lenders										
Issue/Repayment of Loans	-1596	-1860	-234	1	0	-1144	-4162	-1168	19	0
Interest (possibly capitalised before 1883)	-2550	-2077	-1718	-1088	-820	-1328	-1214	-1004	-995	-996
	-4146	-3937	-1952	-1087	-820	-2472	-5376	-2172	-976	-996
Externally generated funds	-33065	-19155	-24021	-34117	-37655	-65215	-175679	-82842	-72683	-69715

SHEEPBRIDGE COAL AND IRON COMPANY LTD
FUNDING 1865-1914

Financing for year to 25 June	1905	1906	1907	1908	1909	1910	1911	1912	1913	1914
Internal Finance										
Operating Profit before interest and depreciation	69008	91254	117964	180250	108238	87364	107409	101035	257803	232524
invested in										
Stock	771	-11002	-6980	11956	-12868	14598	-13281	-11966	13692	12123
Debtors	7580	632	14186	-2041	-11418	-3929	-11367	34207	9185	3632
Creditors	5073	-5298	-4525	-9291	4292	-1945	5752	-11283	2009	-7746
Change in Working Capital	13424	-15668	2681	624	-19994	8724	-18896	10958	24886	8009
Cash Flow from operations	55584	106922	115283	179626	128232	78640	126305	90077	232917	224515
invested in										
Cash & Bank	5310	9960	-25705	6267	-13784	3165	-4038	10101	-1679	37742
Fixed Assets	1475	42038	45284	81643	69319	20167	57844	18900	199887	170881
Free Cash	48799	54924	95704	91716	72697	55308	72499	61076	34709	15892
External Finance										
Shareholders										
Issue of Ordinary Share Capital	0	0	0	0	0	0	0	0	0	132953
Dividends Paid	-47803	-53780	-89633	-89633	-71706	-53780	-71706	-51688	-125486	-143413
	-47803	-53780	-89633	-89633	-71706	-53780	-71706	-51688	-125486	-10460
Lenders										
Issue/Repayment of Loans	0	-149	-5160	-1312	-255	-827	-101	-8932	93584	0
Interest (possibly capitalised before 1883)	-996	-995	-911	-771	-736	-701	-692	-456	-2807	-5432
	-996	-1144	-6071	-2083	-991	-1528	-793	-9388	90777	-5432
Externally generated funds	-48799	-54924	-95704	-91716	-72697	-55308	-72499	-61076	-34709	-15892

SHEEPBRIDGE COAL AND IRON COMPANY LTD
FUNDING 1865-1914

Financing for year to 25 June	Summary 1865-1889	percentage 1865-1889	Summary 1890-1914	percentage 1890-1914	Summary 1865-1914	percentage 1865-1914
Internal Finance						
Operating Profit before interest and depreciation	**689105**	**-247.01**	**2620792**	**178.54**	**3309897**	**278.40**
invested in						
Stock	43434	-15.57	21662	1.48	65096	5.48
Debtors	93481	-33.51	10541	0.72	104022	8.75
Creditors	-60491	21.68	-53570	-3.65	-114061	-9.59
Change in Working Capital	**76424**	**-27.39**	**-21367**	**-1.46**	**55057**	**4.63**
Cash Flow from operations	**612681**	**-219.62**	**2642159**	**180.00**	**3254840**	**273.77**
invested in						
Cash & Bank	161	-0.06	58673	4.00	58834	4.95
Fixed Assets	891498	-319.56	1115603	76.00	2007101	168.82
Free Cash	**-278978**	**100.00**	**1467883**	**100.00**	**1188905**	**100.00**
External Finance						
Shareholders						
Issue of Ordinary Share Capital	610600	-218.87	189718	12.92	800318	67.32
Dividends Paid	-364353	130.60	-1590424	-108.35	-1954777	-164.42
	246247	**-88.27**	**-1400706**	**-95.42**	**-1154459**	**-97.10**
Lenders						
Issue/Repayment of Loans	113932	-40.84	-11849	-0.81	102083	8.59
Interest (possibly capitalised before 1883)	-81201	29.11	-55328	-3.77	-136529	-11.48
	32731	**-11.73**	**-67177**	**-4.58**	**-34446**	**-2.90**
Externally generated funds	**278978**	**-100.00**	**-1467883**	**-100.00**	**-1188905**	**-100.00**

STAVELEY COAL AND IRON COMPANY LTD
FUNDING 1864-1914

Financing for year to 30 June	Incorporated 1863										
	1864	1865	1866	1867	1868	1869	1870	1871	1872	1873	1874
Internal Finance											
Operating Profit before interest and depreciation invested in	31562	81922	81531	72892	75040	89750	78584	77692	100936	282609	280401
Stock	63198	-10246	7452	-1781	-772	-8449	-3329	11525	-12954	19778	-13639
Debtors	84041	12741	-5152	-8276	-4765	19403	-14698	7746	10375	127426	99588
Creditors	-42746	-6575	-31376	7126	-1379	6881	6807	8768	5358	-30801	17221
Change in Working Capital	**104493**	**-4080**	**-29076**	**-2931**	**-6916**	**17835**	**-11220**	**28039**	**2779**	**116403**	**103170**
Cash Flow from operations	**-72931**	**86002**	**110607**	**75823**	**81956**	**71915**	**89804**	**49653**	**98157**	**166206**	**177231**
invested in											
Cash & Bank	48598	-44846	18376	-8833	-7327	-4975	15070	-19878	40778	44394	-55715
Fixed Assets	414737	48903	1119	22747	24117	18252	4337	3334	0	18389	0
Free Cash	**-536266**	**81945**	**91112**	**61909**	**65166**	**58638**	**70397**	**66197**	**57379**	**103423**	**232946**
External Finance											
Shareholders											
Issue of Ordinary Share Capital	240000	176000	0	0	0	0	0	0	0	0	0
Dividends Paid	0	-60620	-91234	-61909	-65166	-48875	-65167	-65167	-65167	-91858	-183091
	240000	**115380**	**-91234**	**-61909**	**-65166**	**-48875**	**-65167**	**-65167**	**-65167**	**-91858**	**-183091**
Lenders											
Issue/Repayment of Loans	296266	-197325	122	0	0	-4063	500	5000	14700	-4950	-46000
Interest (estimated pre 1907 only) (6% pre 1896, 4.5% after)						-5700	-5730	-6030	-6912	-6615	-3855
	296266	**-197325**	**122**	**0**	**0**	**-9763**	**-5230**	**-1030**	**7788**	**-11565**	**-49855**
Externally generated funds	**536266**	**-81945**	**-91112**	**-61909**	**-65166**	**-58638**	**-70397**	**-66197**	**-57379**	**-103423**	**-232946**

STAVELEY COAL AND IRON COMPANY LTD
FUNDING 1864-1914

Financing for year to 30 June	1875	1876	1877	1878	1879	1880	1881	1882	1883	1884	1885
Internal Finance											
Operating Profit before interest and depreciation invested in	152010	99332	86274	50838	40297	60642	66152	60439	61372	51067	45293
Stock	-2432	3187	11172	9410	-5382	-1969	-7290	-4658	-6399	3761	2039
Debtors	-55504	-57988	-56374	-51282	-20095	-2212	7532	-13612	163	-4243	1963
Creditors	-4765	10174	6414	296	-1738	-6063	3767	2955	2631	5453	-4931
Change in Working Capital	-62701	-44627	-38788	-41576	-27215	-10244	4009	-15315	-3605	4971	-929
Cash Flow from operations invested in	214711	143959	125062	92414	67512	70886	62143	75754	64977	46096	46222
Cash & Bank	-7097	-41498	68	7525	14450	5286	-2801	16219	-13666	-7057	10223
Fixed Assets	34674	22142	37865	25293	13956	18977	11804	5455	25563	9410	3699
Free Cash	187134	163315	87129	59596	39106	46623	53140	54080	53080	43743	32300
External Finance											
Shareholders											
Issue of Ordinary Share Capital	0	0	0	0	0	0	0	0	0	0	0
Dividends Paid	-183091	-117924	-72308	-59275	-39725	-46242	-52759	-52759	-52759	-46242	-33209
	-183091	-117924	-72308	-59275	-39725	-46242	-52759	-52759	-52759	-46242	-33209
Lenders											
Issue/Repayment of Loans	-200	-44200	-14500	0	1000	0	0	-1000	0	3000	1500
Interest (estimated pre 1907 only) (6% pre 1896, 4.5% after)	-3843	-1191	-321	-321	-381	-381	-381	-321	-321	-501	-591
	-4043	-45391	-14821	-321	619	-381	-381	-1321	-321	2499	909
Externally generated funds	-187134	-163315	-87129	-59596	-39106	-46623	-53140	-54080	-53080	-43743	-32300

STAVELEY COAL AND IRON COMPANY LTD
FUNDING 1864-1914

Financing for year to 30 June	1886	1887	1888	1889	1890	1891	1892	1893	1894	1895	1896
Internal Finance											
Operating Profit before interest and depreciation	50946	44091	51221	72247	135740	165502	147195	92494	50370	77583	69507
invested in											
Stock	-9108	-2615	-7475	1741	8474	-7867	6400	12715	-229	10026	-5821
Debtors	13652	25784	885	1948	13828	37719	-10558	5414	-30470	-36872	-1284
Creditors	-21670	-5820	18839	-1525	-3572	-12471	-14765	-10011	-2457	2695	-15129
Change in Working Capital	**-17126**	**17349**	**12249**	**2164**	**18730**	**17381**	**-18923**	**8118**	**-33156**	**-24151**	**-22234**
Cash Flow from operations	**68072**	**26742**	**38972**	**70083**	**117010**	**148121**	**166118**	**84376**	**83526**	**101734**	**91741**
invested in											
Cash & Bank	28502	-29136	4489	-6796	12233	4608	31082	-39241	-12148	26422	-1596
Fixed Assets	1494	15835	957	26747	0	-575	30049	25146	49337	28503	43769
Free Cash	**38076**	**40043**	**33526**	**50132**	**104777**	**144088**	**104987**	**98471**	**46337**	**46809**	**49568**
External Finance											
Shareholders											
Issue of Ordinary Share Capital	0	0	0	0	0	0	0	0	0	0	0
Dividends Paid	-33208	-39725	-33208	-46242	-104891	-143992	-104891	-98375	-46241	-46242	-49500
	-33208	**-39725**	**-33208**	**-46242**	**-104891**	**-143992**	**-104891**	**-98375**	**-46241**	**-46242**	**-49500**
Lenders											
Issue/Repayment of Loans	-4550	0	0	-3800	217	8	8	8	9	-492	8
Interest (estimated pre 1907 only	-318	-318	-318	-90	-103	-104	-104	-104	-105	-75	-76
(6% pre 1896, 4.5% after)	**-4868**	**-318**	**-318**	**-3890**	**114**	**-96**	**-96**	**-96**	**-96**	**-567**	**-68**
Externally generated funds	**-38076**	**-40043**	**-33526**	**-50132**	**-104777**	**-144088**	**-104987**	**-98471**	**-46337**	**-46809**	**-49568**

STAVELEY COAL AND IRON COMPANY LTD
FUNDING 1864-1914

Financing for year to 30 June	1897	1898	1899	1900	1901	1902	1903	1904	1905	1906	1907
Internal Finance											
Operating Profit before interest and depreciation invested in	**71115**	**77989**	**153199**	**318650**	**344171**	**151851**	**157657**	**118140**	**153452**	**145112**	**195680**
Stock	-10554	-489	5682	11743	31896	-9915	2566	25229	27453	-21145	-20542
Debtors	33415	18823	32495	64156	45367	-71542	-45877	998	-21678	26939	28669
Creditors	8370	-5191	-4414	-9374	-43415	34109	-10603	-10683	10344	-17696	-4700
Change in Working Capital	**31231**	**13143**	**33763**	**66525**	**33848**	**-47348**	**-53914**	**15544**	**16119**	**-11902**	**3427**
Cash Flow from operations	**39884**	**64846**	**119436**	**252125**	**310323**	**199199**	**211571**	**102596**	**137333**	**157014**	**192253**
invested in											
Cash & Bank	17897	-40965	33758	46004	-63206	6929	54113	-28904	33090	6431	-186960
Fixed Assets	27137	46860	-18891	20095	102618	100344	84722	28908	18501	36107	245859
Free Cash	**-5150**	**58951**	**104569**	**186026**	**270911**	**91926**	**72736**	**102592**	**85742**	**114476**	**133354**
External Finance											
Shareholders											
Issue of Ordinary Share Capital	0	0	0	0	0	0	0	0	0	0	0
Dividends Paid	-56016	-56017	-101634	-183091	-261291	-117925	-78825	-78825	-72308	-111408	-130959
	-56016	**-56017**	**-101634**	**-183091**	**-261291**	**-117925**	**-78825**	**-78825**	**-72308**	**-111408**	**-130959**
Lenders											
Issue/Repayment of Loans	64108	8	8	8	-6992	29976	10541	-20226	-10359	8	8
Interest (estimated pre 1907 only	-2942	-2942	-2943	-2943	-2628	-3977	-4452	-3541	-3075	-3076	-2403
(6% pre 1896, 4.5% after)	**61166**	**-2934**	**-2935**	**-2935**	**-9620**	**25999**	**6089**	**-23767**	**-13434**	**-3068**	**-2395**
Externally generated funds	**5150**	**-58951**	**-104569**	**-186026**	**-270911**	**-91926**	**-72736**	**-102592**	**-85742**	**-114476**	**-133354**

STAVELEY COAL AND IRON COMPANY LTD
FUNDING 1864-1914

Financing for year to 30 June	1908	1909	1910	1911	1912	1913	1914
Internal Finance							
Operating Profit before interest and depreciation	**268817**	**172431**	**144111**	**149734**	**135859**	**401311**	**376116**
invested in							
Stock	34940	2504	974	15418	-49762	25584	22265
Debtors	-40583	-6560	45295	-35163	50441	133411	-5177
Creditors	-26860	-11471	12381	3821	28095	-73108	10665
Change in Working Capital	**-32503**	**-15527**	**58650**	**-15924**	**28774**	**85887**	**27753**
Cash Flow from operations	**301320**	**187958**	**85461**	**165658**	**107085**	**315424**	**348363**
invested in							
Cash & Bank	221145	-4159	-85201	-28570	17086	46487	19244
Fixed Assets	176543	25830	73902	81795	127542	110773	50000
Free Cash	**-96368**	**166287**	**96760**	**112433**	**-37543**	**158164**	**279119**
External Finance							
Shareholders							
Issue of Ordinary Share Capital	293250	0	0	0	0	0	0
Dividends Paid	-208344	-133199	-94710	-108150	-108150	-148472	-269438
	84906	**-133199**	**-94710**	**-108150**	**-108150**	**-148472**	**-269438**
Lenders							
Issue/Repayment of Loans	14031	-30600	0	-2300	151688	-1001	-1000
Interest (estimated pre 1907 only) (6% pre 1896, 4.5% after)	-2569	-2488	-2050	-1983	-5995	-8691	-8681
	11462	**-33088**	**-2050**	**-4283**	**145693**	**-9692**	**-9681**
Externally generated funds	**96368**	**-166287**	**-96760**	**-112433**	**37543**	**-158164**	**-279119**

STAVELEY COAL AND IRON COMPANY LTD
FUNDING 1864-1914

Financing for year to 30 June	Summary 1864-1889	percentage 1864-1889	Summary 1890-1914	percentage 1890-1914	Summary 1864-1914	percentage 1864-1914
Internal Finance						
Operating Profit before interest and depreciation	**2245140**	**168.32**	**4273786**	**171.64**	**6518926**	**170.48**
invested in						
Stock	34765	2.61	117545	4.72	152310	3.98
Debtors	119046	8.92	231206	9.29	350252	9.16
Creditors	-56699	-4.25	-165440	-6.64	-222139	-5.81
Change in Working Capital	**97112**	**7.28**	**183311**	**7.36**	**280423**	**7.33**
Cash Flow from operations	**2148028**	**161.04**	**4090475**	**164.27**	**6238503**	**163.15**
invested in						
Cash & Bank	4353	0.33	85579	3.44	89932	2.35
Fixed Assets	809806	60.71	1514874	60.84	2324680	60.79
Free Cash	**1333869**	**100.00**	**2490022**	**100.00**	**3823891**	**100.00**
External Finance						
Shareholders						
Issue of Ordinary Share Capital	416000	31.19	293250	11.78	709250	18.55
Dividends Paid	-1706930	-127.97	-2912894	-116.98	-4619824	-120.81
	-1290930	**-96.78**	**-2619644**	**-105.21**	**-3910574**	**-102.27**
Lenders						
Issue/Repayment of Loans	1500	0.11	197672	7.94	199172	5.21
Interest (estimated pre 1907 only) (6% pre 1896, 4.5% after)	-44439	-3.33	-68050	-2.73	-112489	-2.94
	-42939	**-3.22**	**129622**	**5.21**	**86683**	**2.27**
Externally generated funds	**-1333869**	**-100.00**	**-2490022**	**-100.00**	**-3823891**	**-100.00**

TREDEGAR IRON AND COAL COMPANY LTD
FUNDING 1882-1914

Financing for year to 31 March	1881	1882	1883	1884	1885	1886	1887	1888	1889	1890	1891	1892
	Incorporated 1873											
	cumulative figures to 1881											
Internal Finance	balancing figure											
Operating Profit before interest and depreciation	85863	65316	60749	9370	47486	55773	22488	20918	35130	84289	65279	24742
invested in												
Stock	92520	2952	21850	-2561	9919	999	-27597	-2502	18085	37129	23362	1845
Debtors	79641	-9303	47152	-29929	-11365	-2295	7681	2782	19702	4391	-2390	-21648
Creditors	-50065	-28593	10034	6001	24651	2365	-8403	-6515	381	-11108	13557	3509
Change in Working Capital	122096	-34944	79036	-26489	23205	1069	-28319	-6235	38168	30412	34529	-16294
Cash Flow from operations	-36233	100260	-18287	35859	24281	54704	50807	27153	-3038	53877	30750	41036
invested in												
Cash & Bank	10118	10568	-13847	-2704	4660	2910	2584	-1109	-3592	1354	5161	-15121
Fixed Assets	984124	62441	46636	-10859	3614	5796	1149	288	4077	760	-3227	942
Free Cash	-1030475	27251	-51076	49422	16007	45998	47074	27974	-3523	51763	28816	55215
External Finance												
Shareholders												
Issue of Ordinary Share Capital	837320	10806	54603	54648	1139	7083	936	199	1393	1873	0	0
Dividends Paid		-32500	-51000	-35000	-14250	-29100	-33950	-16460	-14500	-43666	-34000	-38750
	837320	-21694	3603	19648	-13111	-22017	-33014	-16261	-13107	-41793	-34000	-38750
Lenders												
Issue/Repayment of Loans	193155	4155	58359	-55106	7694	-12474	-3643	-807	28068	1186	18246	-4901
Interest		-9712	-10886	-13964	-10590	-11507	-10417	-10906	-11438	-11156	-13062	-11564
	193155	-5557	47473	-69070	-2896	-23981	-14060	-11713	16630	-9970	5184	-16465
Externally generated funds	1030475	-27251	51076	-49422	-16007	-45998	-47074	-27974	3523	-51763	-28816	-55215

TREDEGAR IRON AND COAL COMPANY LTD
FUNDING 1882-1914

Financing for year to 31 March	1893	1894	1895	1896	1897	1898	1899	1900	1901	1902	1903	1904
Internal Finance												
Operating Profit before interest and depreciation	**-1329**	**26109**	**16698**	**31847**	**19821**	**40497**	**13921**	**112666**	**186059**	**103307**	**103496**	**90563**
invested in												
Stock	-64763	-20926	-26901	112	1455	648	-204	13707	34548	-46266	6078	-9627
Debtors	-808	7616	-12062	-7986	16422	-22367	13461	21071	-6574	7049	-8874	26750
Creditors	10590	-3210	7340	-2018	-9179	5641	-13513	-3270	-14433	10897	-13025	-6878
Change in Working Capital	**-54981**	**-16520**	**-31623**	**-9892**	**8698**	**-16078**	**-256**	**31508**	**13541**	**-28320**	**-15821**	**10245**
Cash Flow from operations	**53652**	**42629**	**48321**	**41739**	**11123**	**56575**	**14177**	**81158**	**172518**	**131627**	**119317**	**80318**
invested in												
Cash & Bank	8846	-9828	1824	-1824	1173	-994	-179	0	0	14325	17830	-13029
Fixed Assets	13036	8153	9205	5083	8403	51852	41731	18639	105015	40496	46666	33226
Free Cash	**31770**	**44304**	**37292**	**38480**	**1547**	**5717**	**-27375**	**62519**	**67503**	**76806**	**54821**	**60121**
External Finance												
Shareholders												
Issue of Ordinary Share Capital	0	0	0	0	0	0	0	0	15942	58	0	0
Dividends Paid	-14583	0	0	-24250	-20208	-10105	-10104	0	-80833	-61826	-41217	-41217
	-14583	**0**	**0**	**-24250**	**-20208**	**-10105**	**-10104**	**0**	**-64891**	**-61768**	**-41217**	**-41217**
Lenders												
Issue/Repayment of Loans	-5371	-33108	-27386	-5350	27153	13083	47058	-51342	7935	-5653	-5212	-10124
Interest	-11816	-11196	-9906	-8880	-8492	-8695	-9579	-11177	-10547	-9385	-8392	-8780
	-17187	**-44304**	**-37292**	**-14230**	**18661**	**4388**	**37479**	**-62519**	**-2612**	**-15038**	**-13604**	**-18904**
Externally generated funds	**-31770**	**-44304**	**-37292**	**-38480**	**-1547**	**-5717**	**27375**	**-62519**	**-67503**	**-76806**	**-54821**	**-60121**

TREDEGAR IRON AND COAL COMPANY LTD
FUNDING 1882-1914

Financing for year to 31 March	1905	1906	1907	1908	1909	1910	1911	1912	1913	1914
Internal Finance										
Operating Profit before interest and depreciation	**95882**	**110759**	**148608**	**213236**	**110420**	**129773**	**140615**	**79708**	**140576**	**168861**
invested in										
Stock	-1934	-1908	746	-12509	1319	3153	2302	11109	2187	963
Debtors	-28477	2815	21921	36105	-7806	-19512	15102	-67333	98791	-4245
Creditors	7659	-21589	-6251	-160	-534	6336	-2038	45836	-61879	-14343
Change in Working Capital	**-22752**	**-20682**	**16416**	**23436**	**-7021**	**-10023**	**15366**	**-10388**	**39099**	**-17625**
Cash Flow from operations	**118634**	**131441**	**132192**	**189800**	**117441**	**139796**	**125249**	**90096**	**101477**	**186486**
invested in										
Cash & Bank	-138	21848	10855	49497	-66523	25348	-15665	20014	-58384	24971
Fixed Assets	48061	63352	67860	65550	124916	65697	65952	19988	93431	61479
Free Cash	**70711**	**46241**	**53477**	**74753**	**59048**	**48751**	**74962**	**49794**	**66430**	**100036**
External Finance										
Shareholders										
Issue of Ordinary Share Capital	0	0	0	0	0	0	0	0	0	0
Dividends Paid	-61826	-41216	-41216	-72130	-72128	-46216	-61824	-82433	-61825	-90678
	-61826	**-41216**	**-41216**	**-72130**	**-72128**	**-46216**	**-61824**	**-82433**	**-61825**	**-90678**
Lenders										
Issue/Repayment of Loans	-1065	3720	-5608	1983	17147	3267	-10468	37011	2377	-1847
Interest	-7820	-8745	-6653	-4606	-4067	-5802	-2670	-4372	-6982	-7511
	-8885	**-5025**	**-12261**	**-2623**	**13080**	**-2535**	**-13138**	**32639**	**-4605**	**-9358**
Externally generated funds	**-70711**	**-46241**	**-53477**	**-74753**	**-59048**	**-48751**	**-74962**	**-49794**	**-66430**	**-100036**

TREDEGAR IRON AND COAL COMPANY LTD
FUNDING 1882-1914

Financing for year to 31 March

	Summary 1881-1889	percentage 1881-1889	Summary 1890-1914	percentage 1890-1914	Summary 1881-1914	percentage 1881-1914
Internal Finance						
Operating Profit before interest and depreciation	403093	46.26	2256403	182.93	2659496	734.35
invested in						
Stock	113665	13.04	-44375	-3.60	69290	19.13
Debtors	104066	11.94	61412	4.98	165478	45.69
Creditors	-50144	-5.75	-72063	-5.84	-122207	-33.74
Change in Working Capital	167587	19.23	-55026	-4.46	112561	31.08
Cash Flow from operations	235506	27.03	2311429	187.39	2546935	703.27
invested in						
Cash & Bank	9588	1.10	21661	1.76	31249	8.63
Fixed Assets	1097266	125.93	1056266	85.63	2153532	594.65
Free Cash	-871348	-100.00	1233502	100.00	362154	100.00
External Finance						
Shareholders						
Issue of Ordinary Share Capital	968127	111.11	17873	1.45	986000	272.26
Dividends Paid	-226760	-26.02	-1052251	-85.31	-1279011	-353.17
	741367	85.08	-1034378	-83.86	-293011	-80.91
Lenders						
Issue/Repayment of Loans	219401	25.18	12731	1.03	232132	64.10
Interest	-89420	-10.26	-211855	-17.18	-301275	-83.19
	129981	14.92	-199124	-16.14	-69143	-19.09
Externally generated funds	871348	100.00	-1233502	-100.00	-362154	-100.00

WIGAN COAL AND IRON COMPANY LTD
FUNDING 1865-1914

Financing for year to 31 December	Incorporated 1864 1865	1866	1867	1868	1869	1870	1871	1872	1873	1874
Internal Finance										
Operating Profit before interest and depreciation	**55358**	**111779**	**138044**	**121558**	**158694**	**209815**	**225319**	**363086**	**476462**	**203889**
invested in										
Stock	48414	-13571	40472	26245	17500	2243	-16766	17128	33970	-66299
Debtors	211554	26030	25107	-21829	33477	23007	9089	38776	36210	-100271
Creditors	-204539	103265	-17561	-2480	16706	10001	-38131	57503	-13677	28719
Change in Working Capital	**55429**	**115724**	**48018**	**1936**	**67683**	**35251**	**-45808**	**113407**	**56503**	**-137851**
Cash Flow from operations	**-71**	**-3945**	**90026**	**119622**	**91011**	**174564**	**271127**	**249679**	**419959**	**341740**
invested in										
Cash & Bank	0	-30764	-13284	22798	27717	-19141	39761	53991	7097	20347
Fixed Assets	1630155	89304	117510	73012	-37093	28692	73074	16615	117472	63659
Free Cash	**-1630226**	**-62485**	**-14200**	**23812**	**100387**	**165013**	**158292**	**179073**	**295390**	**257734**
External Finance										
Shareholders										
Issue of Ordinary Share Capital	1535170	0	49345	120785	0	38200	0	0	0	0
Dividends Paid	0	-73698	-87469	-152859	-62487	-129028	-108584	-162875	-253361	-235264
	1535170	**-73698**	**-38124**	**-32074**	**-62487**	**-90828**	**-108584**	**-162875**	**-253361**	**-235264**
Lenders										
Issue/Repayment of Loans	99535	143900	64735	22639	-23785	-62000	-39572	-7113	-33866	-15416
Interest	-4479	-7717	-12411	-14377	-14115	-12185	-10136	-9085	-8163	-7054
(estimated at 4.5% pre 1881)	**95056**	**136183**	**52324**	**8262**	**-37900**	**-74185**	**-49708**	**-16198**	**-42029**	**-22470**
Externally generated funds	**1630226**	**62485**	**14200**	**-23812**	**-100387**	**-165013**	**-158292**	**-179073**	**-295390**	**-257734**

WIGAN COAL AND IRON COMPANY LTD
FUNDING 1865-1914

Financing for year to 31 December	1875	1876	1877	1878	1879	1880	1881	1882	1883	1884
Internal Finance										
Operating Profit before interest and depreciation	**182460**	**106018**	**93745**	**60465**	**105465**	**88972.**	**110016**	**111994**	**100332**	**105461**
invested in										
Stock	24836	27772	-602	19221	-2374	9242	-27941	10462	19265	19442
Debtors	55029	-23477	9598	22136	21206	17212	16726	34685	3649	18936
Creditors	-14099	7889	9124	1216	-17114	-1882	10422	-11123	1953	2040
Change in Working Capital	**65766**	**12184**	**18120**	**42573**	**1718**	**24572**	**-793**	**34024**	**24867**	**40418**
Cash Flow from operations	**116694**	**93834**	**75625**	**17892**	**103747**	**64400**	**110909**	**77970**	**75465**	**65043**
invested in										
Cash & Bank	-68495	-77055	8645	-34695	68663	-8599	38447	-35132	737	-665
Fixed Assets	30869	25664	53645	36029	27120	31988	22004	41660	27036	8279
Free Cash	**154320**	**145225**	**13335**	**16558**	**7964**	**41011**	**50458**	**71442**	**47692**	**57429**
External Finance										
Shareholders										
Issue of Ordinary Share Capital	0	0	0	0	0	0	0	0	0	0
Dividends Paid	-144778	-108583	-67865	-33931	0	-29407	-9049	-54292	-31670	-40719
	-144778	**-108583**	**-67865**	**-33931**	**0**	**-29407**	**-9049**	**-54292**	**-31670**	**-40719**
Lenders										
Issue/Repayment of Loans	-2900	-30757	61098	25898	1170	-2500	-32561	-9800	-8979	-10100
Interest (estimated at 4.5% pre 1881)	-6642	-5885	-6568	-8525	-9134	-9104	-8848	-7350	-7043	-6610
	-9542	**-36642**	**54530**	**17373**	**-7964**	**-11604**	**-41409**	**-17150**	**-16022**	**-16710**
Externally generated funds	**-154320**	**-145225**	**-13335**	**-16558**	**-7964**	**-41011**	**-50458**	**-71442**	**-47692**	**-57429**

WIGAN COAL AND IRON COMPANY LTD
FUNDING 1865-1914

Financing for year to 31 December	1885	1886	1887	1888	1889	1890	1891	1892	1893	1894
Internal Finance										
Operating Profit before interest and depreciation	**87712**	**59383**	**86804**	**106623**	**146795**	**259781**	**199674**	**173631**	**84863**	**94923**
invested in										
Stock	3419	262	20791	-37756	-27863	12530	-2107	14777	-37044	36216
Debtors	12379	4984	22273	3112	47942	1299	-12346	-26793	-40021	-21104
Creditors	-275	-9034	-26736	47470	-28707	25086	-6615	-523	13368	3225
Change in Working Capital	**15523**	**-3788**	**16328**	**12826**	**-8628**	**38915**	**-21068**	**-12539**	**-63697**	**18337**
Cash Flow from operations	**72189**	**63171**	**70476**	**93797**	**155423**	**220866**	**220742**	**186170**	**148560**	**76586**
invested in										
Cash & Bank	315	144	-115	-415	1191	41022	18971	-24271	37172	-51095
Fixed Assets	12083	22546	38141	70087	81798	43360	20031	59658	23551	65383
Free Cash	**59791**	**40481**	**32450**	**24125**	**72434**	**136484**	**181740**	**150783**	**87837**	**62298**
External Finance										
Shareholders										
Issue of Ordinary Share Capital	0	0	0	0	0	0	0	0	0	0
Dividends Paid	-38456	-13572	-9049	-20359	-54292	-126681	-167399	-126680	-67865	-54292
	-38456	**-13572**	**-9049**	**-20359**	**-54292**	**-126681**	**-167399**	**-126680**	**-67865**	**-54292**
Lenders										
Issue/Repayment of Loans	-15100	-21820	-19000	0	-15000	-7000	-12000	-22500	-19200	-8006
Interest	-6235	-5089	-4401	-3766	-3142	-2803	-2341	-1603	-772	0
(estimated at 4.5% pre 1881)	**-21335**	**-26909**	**-23401**	**-3766**	**-18142**	**-9803**	**-14341**	**-24103**	**-19972**	**-8006**
Externally generated funds	**-59791**	**-40481**	**-32450**	**-24125**	**-72434**	**-136484**	**-181740**	**-150783**	**-87837**	**-62298**

WIGAN COAL AND IRON COMPANY LTD
FUNDING 1865-1914

Financing for year to 31 December	1895	1896	1897	1898	1899	1900	1901	1902	1903	1904
Internal Finance										
Operating Profit before interest and depreciation	**60365**	**76557**	**84658**	**114324**	**247346**	**480439**	**200479**	**128694**	**106681**	**86839**
invested in										
Stock	14035	1353	-5233	-29376	-21935	6835	26207	-22779	25187	3054
Debtors	22702	-21991	-9804	7687	8974	13330	-56361	-10456	-1903	-4215
Creditors	-14686	-11888	-7513	-15726	10547	2619	-3604	3246	9804	-13604
Change in Working Capital	**22051**	**-32526**	**-22550**	**-37415**	**-2414**	**22784**	**-33758**	**-29989**	**33088**	**-14765**
Cash Flow from operations	**38314**	**109083**	**107208**	**151739**	**249760**	**457655**	**234237**	**158683**	**73593**	**101604**
invested in										
Cash & Bank	-10552	41982	22969	22359	43235	138888	-112522	-22197	-101300	12382
Fixed Assets	-901	21858	16375	38894	88893	101599	30057	54200	66309	7785
Free Cash	**49767**	**45243**	**67864**	**90486**	**117632**	**217168**	**316702**	**126680**	**108584**	**81437**
External Finance										
Shareholders										
Issue of Ordinary Share Capital	0	0	0	0	0	0	0	0	0	0
Dividends Paid	-49767	-45243	-67864	-90486	-117632	-217168	-316702	-126680	-108584	-81437
	-49767	**-45243**	**-67864**	**-90486**	**-117632**	**-217168**	**-316702**	**-126680**	**-108584**	**-81437**
Lenders										
Issue/Repayment of Loans	0	0	0	0	0	0	0	0	0	0
Interest										
(estimated at 4.5% pre 1881)	**0**	**0**	**0**	**0**	**0**	**0**	**0**	**0**	**0**	**0**
Externally generated funds	**-49767**	**-45243**	**-67864**	**-90486**	**-117632**	**-217168**	**-316702**	**-126680**	**-108584**	**-81437**

WIGAN COAL AND IRON COMPANY LTD
FUNDING 1865-1914

Financing for year to 31 December	1905	1906	1907	1908	1909	1910	1911	1912	1913	1914
Internal Finance										
Operating Profit before interest and depreciation	**103783**	**43892**	**151703**	**61637**	**87104**	**119672**	**114863**	**153872**	**184602**	**93145**
invested in										
Stock	-28149	3850	28773	-13169	2562	13926	-1855	-73299	56761	20005
Debtors	26262	7198	29836	-35149	-7351	20591	22140	9038	-5141	-2660
Creditors	-12679	-12484	-30968	32990	-534	-22068	14138	-14920	-2185	14805
Change in Working Capital	**-14566**	**-1436**	**27641**	**-15328**	**-5323**	**12449**	**34423**	**-79181**	**49435**	**32150**
Cash Flow from operations	**118349**	**45328**	**124062**	**76965**	**92427**	**107223**	**80440**	**233053**	**135167**	**60995**
invested in										
Cash & Bank	-35876	18658	17324	-42819	-13606	57816	-35003	128714	-29845	-71741
Fixed Assets	81836	-45719	-1845	-24994	38168	-361	43054	22901	47380	51298
Free Cash	**72389**	**72389**	**108583**	**144778**	**67865**	**49768**	**72389**	**81438**	**117632**	**81438**
External Finance										
Shareholders										
Issue of Ordinary Share Capital	0	0	0	0	0	0	0	0	0	0
Dividends Paid	-72389	-72389	-108583	-144778	-67865	-49768	-72389	-81438	-117632	-81438
	-72389	**-72389**	**-108583**	**-144778**	**-67865**	**-49768**	**-72389**	**-81438**	**-117632**	**-81438**
Lenders										
Issue/Repayment of Loans	0	0	0	0	0	0	0	0	0	0
Interest (estimated at 4.5% pre 1881)	0	0	0	0	0	0	0	0	0	0
	0	**0**	**0**	**0**	**0**	**0**	**0**	**0**	**0**	**0**
Externally generated funds	**-72389**	**-72389**	**-108583**	**-144778**	**-67865**	**-49768**	**-72389**	**-81438**	**-117632**	**-81438**

WIGAN COAL AND IRON COMPANY LTD
FUNDING 1865-1914

Financing for year to 31 December	Summary 1865-1889	percentage 1865-1889	Summary 1890-1914	percentage 1890-1914	Summary 1865-1914	percentage 1865-1914
Internal Finance						
Operating Profit before interest and depreciation invested in	**3616350**	**1176.03**	**3513527**	**129.68**	**7129877**	**236.33**
Stock	147512	47.97	31125	1.15	178637	5.92
Debtors	547540	178.06	-86238	-3.18	461302	15.29
Creditors	-89050	-28.96	-40169	-1.48	-129219	-4.28
Change in Working Capital	**606002**	**197.07**	**-95282**	**-3.52**	**510720**	**16.93**
Cash Flow from operations invested in	**3010348**	**978.96**	**3608809**	**133.20**	**6619157**	**219.40**
Cash & Bank	1493	0.49	50665	1.87	52158	1.73
Fixed Assets	2701349	878.47	848770	31.33	3550119	117.68
Free Cash	**307506**	**100.00**	**2709374**	**100.00**	**3016880**	**100.00**
External Finance						
Shareholders						
Issue of Ordinary Share Capital	1743500	566.98	0	0.00	1743500	57.79
Dividends Paid	-1921647	-624.91	-2633149	-97.19	-4554796	-150.98
	-178147	**-57.93**	**-2633149**	**-97.19**	**-2811296**	**-93.19**
Lenders						
Issue/Repayment of Loans	68706	22.34	-68706	-2.54	0	0.00
Interest (estimated at 4.5% pre 1881)	-198065	-64.41	-7519	-0.28	-205584.0825	-6.81
	-129359	**-42.07**	**-76225**	**-2.81**	**-205584**	**-6.81**
Externally generated funds	**-307506**	**-100.00**	**-2709374**	**-100.00**	**-3016880**	**-100.00**